Contents

Base Words and Endings
-ed, -ing

Add **-ing** or **-ed** to each base word to make a new word.
Double the final consonant if you need to. Say the word.
Then write the number of syllables you hear.

1. bag + ing = _____ ___

2. help + ed = _____ ___

3. swim + ing = _____ ___

4. rub + ed = _____ ___

5. trot + ed = _____ ___

Read the sentence. Underline the word that ends with **-ing**
or **-ed**. Then write the base word on the line.

6. Maria played baseball with her pals. _____

7. She batted last on her team. _____

8. She was fast at running the bases. _____

9. Sometimes she missed the ball. _____

10. Maria wanted to be a good player. _____

Naming with Pronouns

The subject of a sentence names the person or thing that does the action of the verb. A **pronoun** can take the place of this noun.

Greg is sick at home.   **Subject** Greg

He is sick at home.   **Pronoun** He

Thinking Question
Which pronoun can take the place of the noun or nouns in the subject?

Write the pronoun that can take the place of the underlined subject. Use the words in the box to help you.

He	She	It	They

1. Lisa has an idea.

_____

2. The students make a card.

_____

3. Ben puts the card in the mailbox.

_____

4. The card makes Greg smile.

_____

5. Greg puts his card on his desk.

_____

Using Pronouns

- Use a **pronoun** to replace a noun that comes after a verb.
- Use these pronouns: *me, him, her, it, us,* and *them.*

Nouns	**Pronouns**
Bob rides a <u>bike</u>.	Bob rides **it.**
I saw <u>Bob</u> in the park.	I saw **him** in the park.
He saw <u>my friends</u>.	He saw **them.**
He talked to <u>Tanya and me</u>.	He talked to **us.**

Thinking Question
Which pronoun can take the place of the noun or nouns after the verb?

Draw a line under the pronoun in ( ) that should take the place of the underlined noun. Write the new sentence.

1. The artist talks to <u>his customers</u>. (them, me)

_____

2. A customer gives <u>Anthony</u> money. (her, him)

_____

3. The artist sells <u>a painting</u>. (it, us)

_____

4. Trisha laughs at <u>Gina and me</u>. (her, us)

_____

Focus Trait: Elaboration Details

Without Details	With Details
He looked at the people.	He looked **out the window** at the **crowd of people shouting and waving.**

A. Read these sentences about *Mr. Tanen's Tie Trouble.*
   Add details to help readers see what is happening.

Without Details	With Details
1. Mr. Tanen was upset.	Mr. Tanen was upset _____ _____
2. Everyone came.	Everyone came _____ _____

B. Read each sentence. Look at the picture on pages 24–25 of
   Mr. Tanen's Tie Trouble. Add your own details to make each
   sentence more interesting. Write your new sentences.

Without Details	With Details
3. Mr. Tanen held up a tie.	
4. The dentist bought a tie.	
5. The ties were nice.	

Naming Yourself Last

Mr. Tanen's Tie Trouble
Grammar: Pronouns

Rewrite each sentence correctly.

1. I and Ann had a picnic by myself.

_____

2. When do she and i need to come in?

_____

3. Yesterday, i played at home by ourselves.

_____

Underline the pronoun that can take the place of the underlined noun or nouns. Then write the new sentence.

4. The team captain picked <u>Caitlin and Eric.</u> (them, we)

_____

5. The coach helped <u>Molly.</u> (she, her)

_____

6. The tall kid hit <u>the ball.</u> (them, it)

_____

Name _____ Date _____

Lesson 16
READER'S NOTEBOOK

Mr. Tanen's Tie Trouble
Vocabulary Strategies:
Homographs

Homographs

Look for words in the sentence that show the meaning of the underlined word. Circle one or more clue words in each sentence. Then circle the correct meaning below the sentence.

1. I gave my mom a <u>present</u> for her birthday.

    gift   not absent

2. Does your baby brother ever <u>rest</u>?

    what is left   go to sleep

3. Are you a <u>pupil</u> in my class?

    student   part of the eye

4. Make a <u>ring</u> around your answer.

    circle   sound of a bell   jewelry for a finger

5. Please take this <u>slip</u> to the office.

    small piece of paper   slide easily

6. Please wait a <u>second</u> and I will answer your question.

    right after the first   part of a minute

Proofread for Spelling

Proofread the paragraph. Circle the eight misspelled
words. Then write the correct spellings on the
lines below.

When my sister went away to school, her cat
mised her. Kitty stoped eating. She started runing in
circles. I didn't know what to do. I claped my hands and
called her name. I tried hoping around. I bated balls
to her. Nothing made her feel better! Finally, I had an
idea. I grabed some of my sister's clothes and put them
in Kitty's bed. Kitty rubed against the clothes. Then she
curled up and started purring!

Spelling Words

**Basic
Words**

1. running
2. clapped
3. stopped
4. hopping
5. batted
6. selling
7. pinned
8. cutting
9. sitting
10. rubbed
11. missed
12. grabbed

1. _____   5. _____

2. _____   6. _____

3. _____   7. _____

4. _____   8. _____

Put the parts of each word in order. Then write the Spelling
Word correctly.

9. nedpin _____

10. lingsel _____

11. ttuingc _____

12. tingsit _____

Kinds of Sentences

Write whether the sentence is a statement, command, or question. Write the sentence correctly on the line.

1. where is the bake sale _____

_____

2. hang this sign _____

_____

3. the money helps the school _____

_____

4. do you like cookies _____

_____

5. share with your sister. _____

_____

6. I like cookies with green icing _____

_____

Connect to Writing

Sentences with Repeated Subjects	Better Sentences
Tony walks to the store. <u>Tony</u> buys milk and eggs.	Tony walks to the store. **He** buys milk and eggs.

Sentences with Repeated Subjects	Better Sentences
Mr. Shay and Mrs. Shay need help shopping. <u>Mr. Shay and Mrs. Shay</u> cannot go to the store.	Mr. Shay and Mrs. Shay need help shopping. **They** cannot go the store.

✎ **Use a pronoun to replace the subject in the underlined sentence. Write the new sentence.**

1. Tony likes to help the Shays. <u>Tony goes to their house each day.</u>

   _____

2. Mrs. Shay likes Tony. <u>Mrs. Shay makes lunch for Tony.</u>

   _____

3. Tony and Mr. Shay sit on the porch. <u>Tony and Mr. Shay play chess.</u>

   _____

4. Tony goes to the store. <u>The store sells good food.</u>

   _____

Long *i* (*i, igh, ie, y*)

Write a word from the box to complete each sentence.

> **Word Bank**
>
> might   pie   kind
> find   night   My

1. Do you like _____ made with fruit?

2. What _____ of pie do you like best?

3. _____ mom will go to the store to get fresh peaches.

4. I _____ go with her.

5. We will _____ the best peaches together.

6. At _____ we will eat peach pie.

Subjects and Verbs

- In a sentence that tells about now, singular subjects use a verb that ends in *-s*.

The teacher (sits) in the bleachers.

- In a sentence that tells about now, plural subjects use a verb without the *-s*.

The teachers (sit) in the bleachers.

Thinking Question
When should I add -s to the end of a verb that tells about now?

✎ **Circle the correct verb to go with the subject. Then rewrite the sentence.**

1. The coaches (ride, rides) the bus to the game.

_____

2. My friend (hand, hands) the man a ticket.

_____

3. Mom and Dad (cheer, cheers) at the game.

_____

4. The players (look, looks) at the goalie.

_____

5. The kicker (kick, kicks) the ball.

_____

Name _____ Date _____

Long *i* (*i*, *igh*, *ie*, *y*)

In each row, circle the words that have the long *i* sound.

1.	by	light	win	pie	pick
2.	ply	swim	mild	fin	slight
3.	milk	child	why	gift	thigh
4.	bright	pink	tie	bind	dry

Write a word from the box that fits each clue.

Word Bank

right   fly   tie
cry   kind

5. This is what a jet does. _____

6. You do this with laces. _____

7. A nice pal is this. _____

8. If you don't go left, you might go this way.

_____

9. A child might do this when he or she is sad.

_____

Name _____ Date _____

Long *i* (*i, igh, y*)

Luke Goes to Bat
Spelling: Long *i* (*i, igh, y*)

Sort the Spelling Words. Put words with the long *i* sound spelled *i*, *igh*, and *y* under the correct baseball glove.

Spelling Words

Basic Words
1. night
2. kind
3. spy
4. child
5. light
6. find
7. right
8. high
9. wild
10. July
11. fry
12. sigh

Review Words
13. by
14. why

i   *igh*   *y*

1. _____   5. _____   10. _____

2. _____   6. _____   11. _____

3. _____   7. _____   12. _____

4. _____   8. _____   13. _____

                 9. _____   14. _____

Circle the letter or letters in each word that spell the long *i* sound.

Subjects and More Verbs

In a sentence that tells about now,
add -es to a verb that ends in *s, sh, ch, tch,*
z, or *x* to match a singular subject.

Thinking Question
When should I add -es
to the end of a verb that
tells about now?

The trains pass the rink.   The train passes the rink.

The girls watch the skaters.   The girl watches the skaters.

The chefs mix hot soup.   The chef mixes hot soup.

The boys reach for a ball.   The boy reaches for a ball.

Draw a line under each correct sentence.

1. The coach fix the skates.

The coach fixes the skates.

2. The kids dash around the rink.

The kids dashes around the rink.

3. The teacher teaches them a trick.

The teacher teach them a trick.

4. Dad misses a turn.

Dad miss a turn.

5. Mom watch from the stands.

Mom watches from the stands.

Focus Trait: Development Using Dialogue

Without Dialogue	With Dialogue
Dani wanted to go to the baseball game.	Dani begged, "Mom, please let me go to the baseball game. Please!"

A. Rewrite each sentence. Use dialogue.

Without Dialogue	With Dialogue
1. Dani asked Mom about the score.	"_____?" Dani asked Mom.
2. Mom told her it was tied.	"_____," Mom said.

B. Rewrite each sentence. Use dialogue.

Sentence	Dialogue
3. Tad told Dani she couldn't play.	
4. Dani wanted to know why.	
5. Tad said she was too young.	

Cumulative Review

Combine a word from the box with a word below. Write the word on the line, and read the whole compound word.

Word Bank

be	box	hive
cake	boat	ball
end	light	

1. pan _____

2. sun _____

3. bee _____

4. base _____

5. may _____

6. week _____

7. sand _____

8. sail _____

Circle two compound words in each sentence. Draw a line between the two words that make up each compound word.

9. We like to look for pinecones in the sunshine.

10. She put on her raincoat and went outside.

Name _____   Date _____

Reader's Guide

Luke Goes to Bat

Luke's Game-Day Journal

A journal lets you tell what happens in your day and share your feelings. Finish Luke's journal, using ideas from the text.

Read pages 54–55. Imagine you are Luke. Write in Luke's journal about this day.

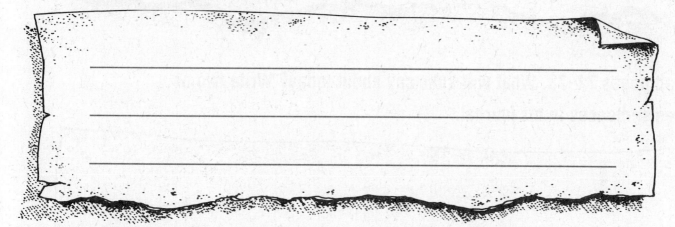

Read pages 58–60. Imagine you are Luke. Write in Luke's journal about this day.

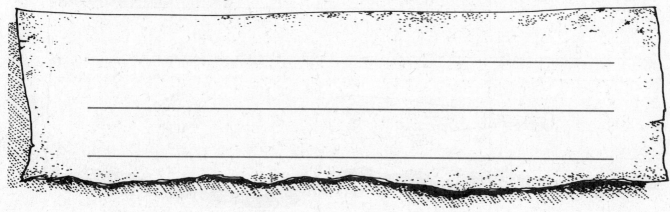

Name _____   Date _____

Read pages 63–65. What is important about this day?
Write two or three sentences in Luke's journal.

_____

_____

_____

_____

Read pages 72–73. What will Luke say about today? Write two or
three sentences in his journal.

_____

_____

_____

_____

Kinds of Sentences

Read each sentence. Tell whether it is a statement, an exclamation, a command, or a question. Then write the sentence correctly on the line.

1. did you hit that ball _____

_____

2. you did a great job _____

_____

3. try that again _____

_____

4. Hanna pitches the ball _____

_____

5. her dad hits the ball _____

_____

6. how far did he hit it _____

_____

Connect to Writing

Subject and Verb Don't Match	Subject and Verb Match
<u>Jared pitch</u> the ball.	<u>Jared pitches</u> the ball.
<u>She swing</u> the bat.	<u>She swings</u> the bat.

Proofread the paragraphs. Find five places where the subject and verb do not match. Write the corrected sentences on the lines below.

Mike play baseball with me. He pitches the ball.
I hit the ball. It get dark out. Mom call me. She yells,
"Dinner!"

I wave at Mike. He wave back. He rush home, too.

1. _____

2. _____

3. _____

4. _____

5. _____

Name _____ Date _____

Long *e* Sound for *y*

Circle the word that tells about each picture. Then use the words to complete the sentences below.

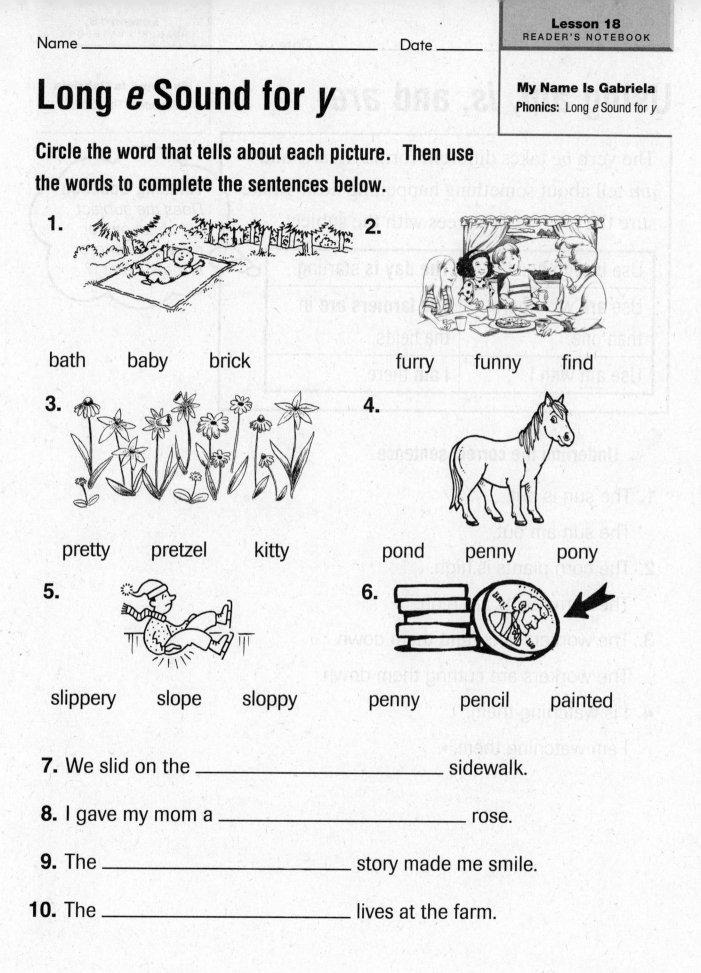

1. bath   baby   brick

2. furry   funny   find

3. pretty   pretzel   kitty

4. pond   penny   pony

5. slippery   slope   sloppy

6. penny   pencil   painted

7. We slid on the _____ sidewalk.

8. I gave my mom a _____ rose.

9. The _____ story made me smile.

10. The _____ lives at the farm.

Using *am*, *is*, and *are*

The verb *be* takes different forms. *Is, are,* and *am* tell about something happening now. Make sure the form of *be* agrees with the subject.

Use **is** with one.	**The day is** starting.
Use **are** with more than one.	**The farmers are** in the fields.
Use **am** with I.	**I am** there.

Thinking Question
Does the subject tell about one or more than one, or is the subject I?

✏️ **Underline the correct sentence.**

1. The sun is out.

   The sun am out.

2. The corn plants is high.

   The corn plants are high.

3. The workers is cutting them down.

   The workers are cutting them down.

4. I is watching them.

   I am watching them.

Using *was* and *were*

> The verb **be** takes different forms. **Was** and
> **were** tell about something that happened in
> the past. Make sure the form of **be** agrees with
> the subject.
>
> | Use **was** with one. | The **market was** busy. |
> |---|---|
> | Use **were** with more than one. | **Papa and Emelina were** shopping. |

Thinking Question
Does the subject tell about one or more than one, or is the subject I?

✐ **Write each sentence correctly.**

1. Mama (was, were) cooking.

_____

2. The beans (was, were) boiling.

_____

3. The rice (was, were) done.

_____

4. We (was, were) hungry.

_____

Focus Trait: Elaboration Using Sense Words

Without Sense Words	With Sense Words
I took off my glove and touched the snow.	I took off my glove and touched the cold, white snow.

Read each description. Use sense words to fill in the blanks.

Without Sense Words	With Sense Words
1. I drank some juice.	I drank some juice that tasted like _____.
2. The barn was filled with pigs.	The barn was filled with _____ pigs.

Pair/Share Work with a partner to add sense words.

Without Sense Words	With Sense Words
3. I saw a field.	
4. She laughed.	
5. I ate a pickle.	

Name _____   Date _____

Changing *y* to *i*

Read the word. Then change *y* to *i* and add *es* to make the word mean more than one. Write the new word.

1.

pony   _____

2.

puppy   _____

3.

baby   _____

Write two sentences with the words that you wrote.

4. _____

5. _____

My Name Is Gabriela

Make an Invitation

Garbriela Mistral is a famous writer who won an award for her writing. Gather some details about her life.

Read pages 92–95. Does Gabriela Mistral have a good imagination? How can you tell?

_____

_____

_____

Read pages 100–101. Gabriela Mistral liked to play school. Do you think she was a good pretend teacher? How can you tell?

_____

_____

Read pages 103 and 107. Did Gabriela Mistral still have a good imagination after she grew up? How can you tell?

_____

_____

Using *Being* Verbs

🖉 **Underline the correct sentence.**

1. The rodeo is here.

The rodeo are here.

The rodeo am here.

2. The crowds is clapping.

The crowds are clapping.

The crowds am clapping.

🖉 **Write each sentence correctly.**

3. Gabriela (was, were) a teacher.

_____

4. She (was, were) speaking.

_____

5. Her students (was, were) listening.

_____

6. They (was, were) learning a lot.

_____

Name _____ Date _____

Lesson 18
READER'S NOTEBOOK

My Name Is Gabriela
Vocabulary Strategies:
Suffixes -y and -ful

Suffixes *-y* and *-ful*

Read each sentence. Add the suffix *-y* or *-ful* to complete the underlined word.

1. The garden smells <u>flower</u> + _____.

2. Joel's smile showed he was <u>joy</u> + _____.

3. The <u>play</u> + _____ kitten

   knocked over a vase.

Circle the word that correctly completes each sentence.

4. I always look both ways before crossing the street.

   I am very _____.

   careful   **carefully**

5. The weather was bad today.

   It was very _____.

   rainful   **rainy**

6. My lemonade was _____ after
   the ice in it melted.

   watery   **waterful**

Proofread for Spelling

**Proofread Tony's letter. Circle six misspelled words.
Then write each misspelled word correctly.**

Dear Grandma and Grandpa,

     Last Friday, I got a new puppe. I was veray

surprised! Dad and Mom let me carey her home. She

was the onlee one I really liked. I'm going to name her

Peny. Don't you think that's a prettie name?

Love,
Tony

1. _____	4. _____
2. _____	5. _____
3. _____	6. _____

Spelling Words

**Basic
Words**
1. happy
2. pretty
3. baby
4. very
5. puppy
6. funny
7. carry
8. lucky
9. only
10. sunny
11. penny
12. city

Write the Basic Word that answers each question.

7. I am very young. What am I? _____.

8. When I feel like this, I laugh. How do I feel? _____.

9. It is warm outside. How is the weather? _____.

10. Where do you see big buildings? _____.

Writing Quotations

✏️ **Underline the correct sentence.**

1. Dad said, "It snowed."

Dad said "it snowed."

2. I asked, may I play outside?

I asked, "May I play outside?"

3. Mom said "have fun!"

Mom said, "Have fun!"

✏️ **Read each paragraph. Then write each paragraph**
correctly. Fix five mistakes in capitalization and punctuation.

The cook said "i will make corn. He put corn
in the bag.

Mama said "I will cook rice. She put rice in
the bag.

_____

_____

_____

_____

Connect to Writing

Sentences with Repeated Subjects	Sentences with Combined Subjects
The weather is rainy. The weather is cool.	The weather is rainy and cool.

Sentences with Repeated Subjects	Sentences with Combined Subjects
The students are reading. The students are learning.	The students are reading and learning.

Combine the sentences with repeating subjects.

Write the new sentence on the line.

1. The animals are eating. The animals are sleeping.

_____

2. They were running. They were playing.

_____

3. Sasha was reading. Sasha was writing.

_____

4. The country is growing. The country is changing.

_____

5. I am chatting. I am laughing.

_____

Words with *ar*

Circle the word that completes each sentence. Then write the word on the line.

1. Dee saw a bright _____ in the sky.

   state   **star**   **sat**

2. The dog in the yard started to _____.

   bark   **dark**   **bank**

3. The children played baseball at the _____.

   part   **paint**   **park**

4. Mom put milk in her shopping _____.

   charm   **chair**   **cart**

5. The cows go into the _____ at night.

   barn   **bean**   **brain**

6. Max is a _____ boy.

   smack   **smart**   **start**

Write two sentences. Use words spelled with *ar*.

7. _____

8. _____

Words with *ar*

Sort the Spelling Words by the number of letters in each word.

3   4   5

1. _____

2. _____

3. _____

4. _____

5. _____

6. _____

7. _____

8. _____

9. _____

10. _____

11. _____

12. _____

13. _____

14. _____

Now, add to your lists. Add two *ar* words you know to each column.

15. _____   17. _____   19. _____

16. _____   18. _____   20. _____

Spelling Words

Basic Words

1. car
2. dark
3. arm
4. star
5. park
6. yard
7. party
8. hard
9. farm
10. start
11. part
12. spark

Review Words

13. art
14. jar

Commas with Place Names

The Signmaker's Assistant

Grammar: Commas in Dates and Places

Use a **comma (,)** between the name of a city or town and the name of a state.

The gas station is in Dallas, Texas.

Thinking Question
Which word is the name of the city or town, and which word is the name of the state?

Write the city and state named in each sentence.
Put a comma in the correct place.

1. The car breaks down after we leave Austin Texas.

_____

2. A truck tows the car to San Antonio Texas.

_____

3. A repairman calls a shop in Miami Florida.

_____

4. The shop sends car parts from Atlanta Georgia.

_____

5. Then we drive to Oakland California.

_____

Name _____ Date _____

Focus Trait: Organization Beginning, Middle, End

Read the story below. Think about the beginning, middle, and end. Then write what each part tells you.

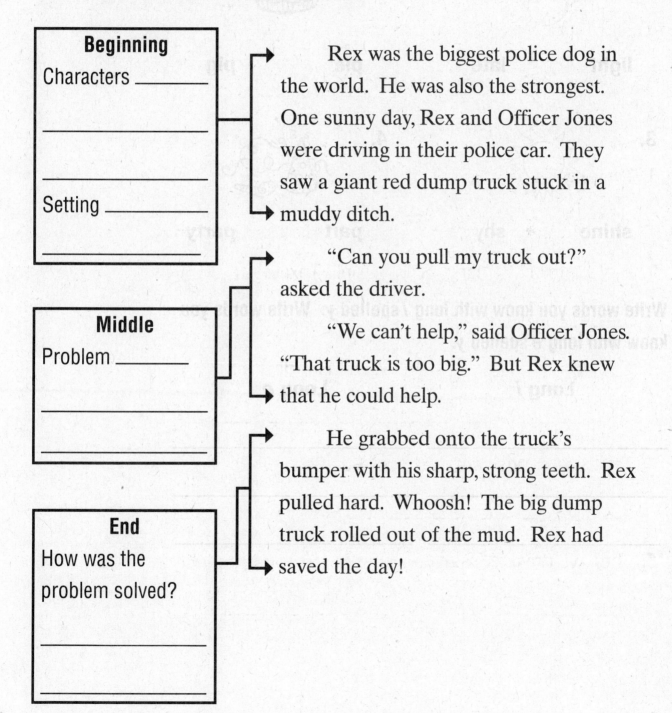

Beginning
Characters _____

_____

_____

Setting _____

_____

Rex was the biggest police dog in the world. He was also the strongest. One sunny day, Rex and Officer Jones were driving in their police car. They saw a giant red dump truck stuck in a muddy ditch.

Middle
Problem _____

_____

_____

"Can you pull my truck out?" asked the driver.

"We can't help," said Officer Jones. "That truck is too big." But Rex knew that he could help.

End
How was the problem solved?

_____

_____

He grabbed onto the truck's bumper with his sharp, strong teeth. Rex pulled hard. Whoosh! The big dump truck rolled out of the mud. Rex had saved the day!

Cumulative Review

Circle the word that goes with each picture. Underline
the letters that spell the long *i* or long *e* sound.

1.

    light   late

2.

    pie   pig

3.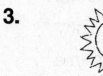

    shine   shy

4.

    part   party

Write words you know with long *i* spelled *y*. Write words you
know with long *e* spelled *y*.

   Long *i*   **Long *e***

_____   _____

_____   _____

Shades of Meaning

Choose the best word from the Word Bank to complete each sentence. Use every word.

Word Bank

tumble	slide	slip

1. The wall of mud began to _____ slowly down the hill.

2. Be careful not to _____ on the slimy seaweed!

3. Turning over and over, the child began to

_____ down the grassy hill.

Word Bank

cool	cold	frozen

4. A _____ breeze is welcome after the day's heat.

5. You should wear a hat on a _____ and snowy day.

6. When the pond is _____, we can skate on it.

Name _____ Date _____

Proofread for Spelling

Proofread the invitation. Circle the six misspelled words. Then write the correct spellings on the lines below.

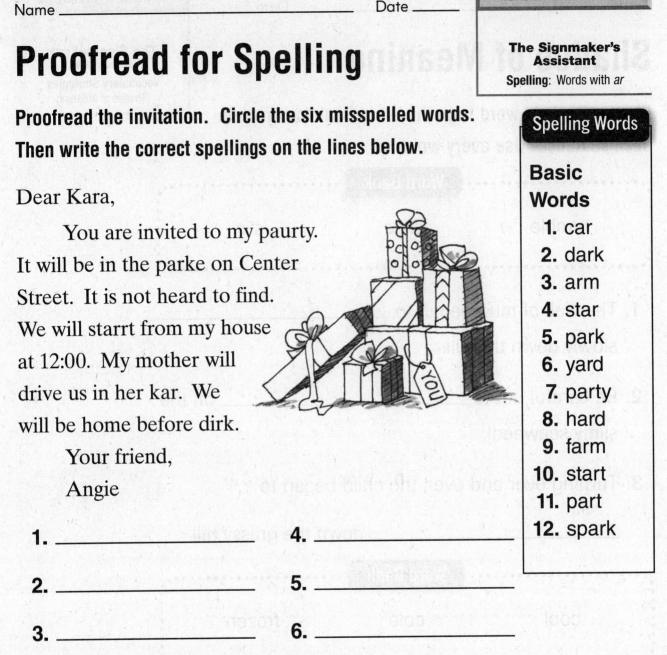

Dear Kara,

   You are invited to my paurty. It will be in the parke on Center Street. It is not heard to find. We will starrt from my house at 12:00. My mother will drive us in her kar. We will be home before dirk.

   Your friend,
   Angie

Spelling Words
Basic Words
1. car
2. dark
3. arm
4. star
5. park
6. yard
7. party
8. hard
9. farm
10. start
11. part
12. spark

1. _____   4. _____

2. _____   5. _____

3. _____   6. _____

Write these other Spelling Words in ABC order: *part, star, yard, farm, arm, spark.*

7. _____   10. _____

8. _____   11. _____

9. _____   12. _____

Writing Proper Nouns

✏️ **Write the name of each underlined word correctly.**

1. The store is closed on <u>thursday</u>.

_____

2. That day is <u>thanksgiving</u>.

_____

3. They put up a sign early in <u>november</u>.

_____

✏️ **Read the paragraphs. Write words from the box to tell when.**

Word Box
July
every Saturday
next Sunday
Mother's Day
Father's Day

My mom loves _____.

The holiday is _____. She wants

flowers. Dad buys them at Lou's Flower Shop.

Mom's birthday is in _____.

Dad loves _____. He wants

to sleep late. Mom says he gets to sleep late

_____!

Connect to Writing

Not Correct	Correct
The sports shop opened on May 8 1998.	The sports shop opened on <u>May 8</u>, <u>1998</u>.

Not Correct	Correct
The soccer ball was made in Detroit Michigan.	The soccer ball was made in <u>Detroit</u>, <u>Michigan</u>.

Proofread the sentences for missing commas. Rewrite each sentence correctly.

1. The sports store opened on March 15 2015.

_____

2. It is in Charleston South Carolina.

_____

3. Mr. Thomas sold ice skates on December 1 2016.

_____

4. He sold beach balls on June 5 2015.

_____

5. He sold shells from Daytona Beach Florida.

_____

Words with *or, ore*

Write words to complete the sentences. Use words from the box.

porch	adore
story	Sport
more	before

1. This is a _____ about my dog.

2. His name is _____.

3. He sleeps on the _____.

4. We play _____ I go to school.

5. After school, we play some _____.

6. I _____ my dog!

Name _____   Date _____

Commas in a Series of Nouns

- A **series of nouns** is three or more nouns that appear together in a sentence.
- Use a comma after each noun in the series except for the last noun.

Sparky, Spike, Rover, and Leo are dogs.

Thinking Question
Are there three or more nouns being listed in a series?

Find the correct sentences. Circle the commas in each correct sentence.

1. Mom Dad, and Kim care for the dogs.

   Mom, Dad, and Kim care for the dogs.

   Mom, Dad, and, Kim, care for the dogs.

2. Dogs, cats, and birds are great pets.

   Dogs cats and birds are great pets.

   Dogs, cats, and, birds are great pets.

3. Max, Harry, and, Grace are puppies.

   Max, Harry, and Grace are puppies.

   Max, Harry, and Grace, are puppies.

4. Puppies need food, water, and, love.

   Puppies need food water and, love.

   Puppies need food, water, and love.

Name _____ Gianncarlo _____ Date ___

Proofread for Spelling

Dex: The Heart of a Hero
Spelling: Words with *or, ore*

Proofread the ad. Cross out the five misspelled words.
Then write the correct spellings in the margin.

Come to our grocery stour!

Big sale on korn!

The sale begins at 8:00 in the mourning.

Sale items are in shart supply.

They won't last long!

Don't furget!

Unscramble the letters to spell a Basic Word.

Write the word on the line.

1. rnbo _____

2. orkf _____

3. soreh _____

4. hnor _____

5. erot _____

6. styor _____

7. crose _____

Spelling Words

Basic Words
1. horn
2. story
3. fork
4. score
5. store
6. corn
7. morning
8. shore
9. short
10. born
11. tore
12. forget

Writing Book Titles

 Rewrite each sentence. Write the book titles correctly. Remember to use capital letters when needed.

1. My favorite book is the cat in the hat.

_____

2. Did Dr. Rames write the book taking care of pets?

_____

 Fix the mistakes in the paragraph. Write the paragraph correctly.

Mr. Grady owns a book store. Today, Lynn buys the book caring for dogs. Mr. Grady also sells her another book. This one is called how to keep a bird.

_____

_____

_____

How Things Look

An **adjective** is a word that tells how something looks.

Adjectives can tell size, color, shape, or how many.

Penguins look short.

Thinking Question
Which word tells more about how something looks?

✏️ **Write the adjective from the box that best fits each sentence. Use the clues in ( ).**

round	small	four	black

1. I see _____ penguins on the ice.
   (tell how many)

2. The penguins stand in a _____ circle.
   (tell shape)

3. They are _____ and white. (tell color)

4. The baby penguin is _____. (tell size)

Name _____ Date _____

Words with *er*

Put the letters together to write a word with *er*.

1. f + a + t + h + er = _____

2. c + o + m + p + u + t + er = _____

3. w + h + i + s + k + er + s = _____

4. t + o + a + s + t + er = _____

5. b + a + k + er = _____

Now use the *er* words you wrote to complete the sentences below.

6. I put my bread in the _____.

7. My cat has long _____ on her face.

8. The _____ sells cookies and pies.

9. I eat dinner with my mother and _____.

10. I play games on the _____.

Words with *er*

Sort the Spelling Words.

Spelling Words

Words that end in *er*

1. _____
2. _____
3. _____
4. _____
5. _____
6. _____
7. _____
8. _____
9. _____
10. _____

Words with *er* in middle

11. _____
12. _____
13. _____
14. _____

Basic Words
1. father
2. over
3. under
4. herd
5. water
6. verb
7. paper
8. cracker
9. offer
10. cover
11. germ
12. master

Review Words
13. fern
14. ever

Underline the letter or letters that make the *er* sound in each word.

How Things Taste and Smell

Penguin Chick
Grammar: What Is an Adjective?

Adjectives can tell how something tastes.
Adjectives can also tell how something smells.

The ocean smells fishy.
The water tastes salty.

Thinking Question
Which word tells more about how something tastes or smells?

Find the adjective in each sentence. The adjective tells more about the underlined word. Write the adjective.

1. The penguins eat the tasty <u>fish</u>.

_____

2. They drink the salty <u>water</u>.

_____

3. The penguins like smelly <u>seafood</u>.

_____

4. They smell the fresh <u>air</u>.

_____

5. They love the taste of sweet <u>squid</u>.

_____

Focus Trait: Elaboration Using Exact Words

Without Exact Words	With Exact Words
In Antarctica there is <u>nothing</u> to build a nest with.	In Antarctica there are **no twigs, leaves, grass, or mud** to build a nest with.

A. Read each sentence. Replace each underlined word with more exact words.

Without Exact Words	With Exact Words
1. The egg stays <u>comfortable</u> in the brood patch.	The egg stays _____ in the brood patch.
2. The penguin fathers <u>are</u> together in a group.	The penguin fathers _____ together in a group.

B. Pair/Share Work with a partner to brainstorm exact words to replace the underlined words in the sentence.

Without Exact Words	With Exact Words
3. With his <u>mouth</u>, the penguin father <u>puts</u> the egg onto his <u>feet</u>.	
4. After the chick <u>comes out of the egg</u>, its wet feathers <u>change</u>.	

87

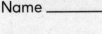

Penguin Chick
Phonics: Words with *ir, ur*

Words with *ir, ur*

1. Write **X** on the bigger **bird**.

Write **bird**.

_____

2. Draw stripes on the **shirt**.

Write **shirt**.

_____

3. Color the one we can **burn** to

make light. Write **burn**.

_____

4. Circle the **birthday** cake.

Write **birthday**.

_____

5. Write **X** on Thursday.

Write **Thursday**.

October

Monday	Tuesday	Wednesday	Thursday	Friday
		1	2	3

_____

Dictionary Entry

Read each sentence. Use the dictionary entries to help you decide what the word means. Write the definition on the line.

---

creature **1.** an animal **2.** a strange or imaginary living thing

shuffle **1.** to walk without picking up your feet **2.** to mix cards or papers so they are in a different order

swallow[1] to make food or drink go down your throat

swallow[2] a small bird with pointed wings and a tail with two points

webbed **1.** having skin that connects the toes or fingers **2.** made of something that looks or feels like a web: *My purse has a webbed strap.*

---

1. Kim had to <u>swallow</u> her food before she could talk.

_____

2. I will <u>shuffle</u> the cards before we start the game.

_____

3. We saw a silly blue <u>creature</u> on TV.

_____

4. Frogs have <u>webbed</u> feet to help them swim and hop.

_____

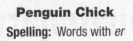

Proofread for Spelling

Penguin Chick
Spelling: Words with *er*

Circle the misspelled words in the items below. Then write the correct spellings on the lines.

Make a Good Snack

1. Wash your hands with soap and wotter. You do not want to get a jerm on your snack.

    _____   _____

2. Cuver a craker with peanut butter. Place another one on top.

    _____   _____

3. Put a payper napkin undr your snack. Pour a glass of milk.

    _____   _____

4. You are now the mayster of snacks! Why not ofer one to your mother or fathr?

    _____ _____ _____

Spelling Words

Basic Words
1. father
2. over
3. under
4. herd
5. water
6. verb
7. paper
8. cracker
9. offer
10. cover
11. germ
12. master

Unscramble the letters to spell a Basic Word.

5. berv _____   7. dher _____

6. ervo _____

Reflexive Pronouns

Circle the correct pronoun to complete each sentence.
Then write the sentence.

1. I bought (ourselves, myself) a book about the South Pole.

_____

2. My partner and I wrote a report by (ourselves, myself).

_____

3. We taught (ourselves, myself) a lot about penguins.

_____

4. I surprised (ourselves, myself) by how much I learned.

_____

5. The teacher said we should be very pleased with
(ourselves, myself).

_____

Connect to Writing

Short, Choppy Sentences	Longer, Smooth Sentence
The penguins were hungry. The penguins were tired.	The penguins were hungry and tired.

Read each pair of sentences. Join the sentences using and between the two adjectives. Write the new sentence.

1. The penguin was cold.

   The penguin was wet.

   _____

2. The rain was heavy.

   The rain was pounding.

   _____

3. The egg was warm.

   The egg was covered.

   _____

4. The sky was cloudy.

   The sky was dark.

   _____

Homophones

**Read the two homophones in each box. Then choose the word
that goes on each line. Read the completed sentences.**

1. I _____ my bike on

a bumpy _____.

| rode |
| road |

2. Let's _____ at the

store to buy _____.

| meat |
| meet |

3. Sam read a _____ about

a dog wagging its _____.

| tale |
| tail |

4. I can _____ the waves of the

_____ crashing on the shore.

| sea |
| see |

5. Jason is _____ from

being sick all _____.

| weak |
| week |

Adjectives

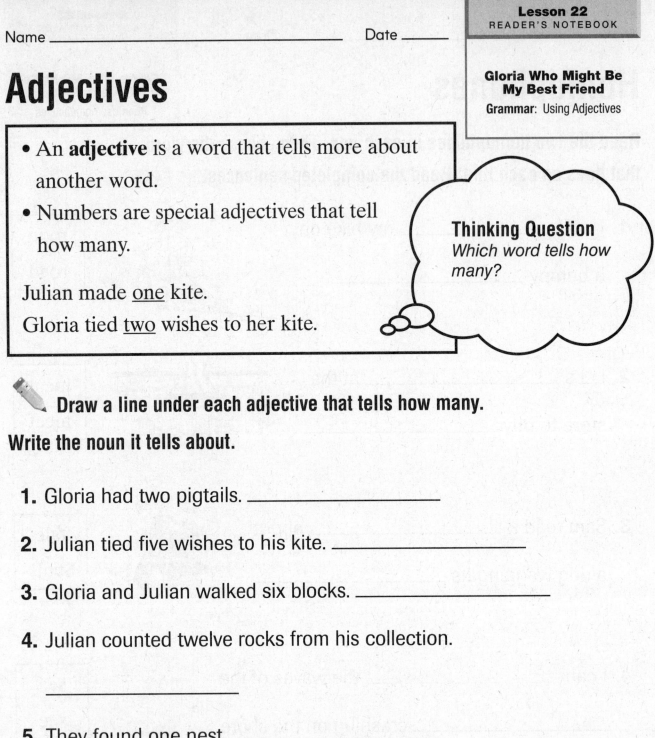

- An **adjective** is a word that tells more about another word.
- Numbers are special adjectives that tell how many.

Julian made <u>one</u> kite.

Gloria tied <u>two</u> wishes to her kite.

Thinking Question
Which word tells how many?

Draw a line under each adjective that tells how many.

Write the noun it tells about.

1. Gloria had two pigtails. _____

2. Julian tied five wishes to his kite. _____

3. Gloria and Julian walked six blocks. _____

4. Julian counted twelve rocks from his collection.

_____

5. They found one nest. _____

Homophones

Choose a word from the box to complete each sentence.
Write the word on the line. Read each completed sentence.

Word Bank

be	blew	rode	weak	two
bee	main	road	sea	too
blue	mane	week	see	

1. The wind _____ the door open.

2. Please save _____ seats at lunch.

3. This flower has a _____ on it!

4. Tim _____ his dad's bike.

5. There are seven days in one _____.

6. I like to swim in the salty _____.

7. What is the _____ idea on that page?

8. There is _____ much noise.

9. My favorite color is _____.

10. It is too dark to _____.

Homophones

Write the Spelling Word that sounds the same as the given word.

1. sea _____

2. bee _____

3. week _____

4. two _____

5. meet _____

6. tail _____

7. mane _____

Now sort the Spelling Words by vowel sounds. The first one is done for you.

Long *e*	Long *a*	*oo* sound
sea	_____	_____
_____	_____	_____
_____	_____	
_____		
_____		
_____		

Spelling Words
Basic Words
1. meet
2. meat
3. week
4. weak
5. mane
6. main
7. tail
8. tale
9. be
10. bee
11. too
12. two
Review Words
13. sea
14. see

Name _____ Date _____

Adjectives with -*er* and -*est*

- Add -er to adjectives to compare **two** people, animals, places, or things.
- Add -est to compare **more than two** people, animals, places, or things.

Jan is tall.

Beth is taller than Jan.

Nina is the tallest friend of all.

Thinking Question
How many people, animals, places, or things are being compared?

✏ **Write the correct word for each sentence.**

1. Beth is _____ than Nina.
    (quieter   quietest)

2. Jan is the _____ person of all.
    (quieter   quietest)

3. Nina has _____ hair than Jan.
    (shorter   shortest)

4. Jan has the _____ hair in the class.
    (longer   longest)

5. Jan has a _____ dog than Nina.
    (smaller   smallest)

Lesson 22
READER'S NOTEBOOK

Gloria Who Might Be My Best Friend
Writing: Informative Writing

Focus Trait: Evidence Details

A. Read each paragraph. Cross out the detail that does not support the main idea. Circle the connecting words.

1. Gloria and Julian are different in some ways.

   They both know how to fly a kite.

   Gloria is a fast runner, but Julian runs slowly.

   Gloria can turn a cartwheel, but Julian can't.

2. Gloria and Julian are alike in some ways.

   Julian knows the best way to make wishes, but Gloria doesn't.

   They like playing outside.

   They go to the same school.

B. Read each main idea. Give a detail that supports the main idea.

Pair/Share Work with a partner to brainstorm possible details for each main idea.

Main Idea	Detail
3. Doctors and nurses are alike in many ways.	
4. Cats and dogs are alike in some ways.	

Using Adjectives

Draw a line under the word in ( ) that correctly completes each sentence.

1. Luis is (a, an) pal.

2. He goes on (a, an) airplane to visit George.

3. George cleans (a, an) attic upstairs.

4. Luis stays for (a, an) week.

5. The boys play in (an, the) park.

Write the correct word for each sentence.

6. The pond is _____ than the pool.
(deeper   deepest)

7. Luis is the _____ swimmer of all.
(faster   fastest)

8. Monday was _____ than Sunday.
(warmer   warmest)

9. January was the _____ month of the ____.
(colder   coldest)

10. George is _____ than Luis.
(older   oldest)

Idioms

**Read each sentence. Choose the meaning from the
box that could replace the underlined words. Write the
meaning on the line.**

Meanings

stay cheerful   very special to him   understands what to do
does her best   tight and uncomfortable

1. Kim's grandpa is proud of her. She is <u>the apple of his eye</u>.

_____

2. Sally has been at her job for a long time, so she

<u>knows the ropes</u>.

_____

3. Jen had a good day at school. She always <u>puts her</u>

<u>best foot forward</u>.

_____

4. Jay is sad, so Mel told him to <u>keep his chin up</u>.

_____

5. I am so nervous! My stomach is <u>tied in knots</u>.

_____

Name _____   Date _____

Lesson 22
READER'S NOTEBOOK

Gloria Who Might Be
My Best Friend
Spelling: Homophones

Proofread for Spelling

Proofread the letter. Circle the misspelled words. Then write the correct spellings on the lines below.

Dear Jen,

    We moved into our new house. It is on Mane Street. We have too trees in the yard. I wanted to climb one, but Mom said it was two week.

    Lucky likes our new yard. He runs around and wags his tale. That silly dog bit at a be. I wonder if he thought it was meet to eat.

    This weak I start my new school. I hope I'll meat someone who wants to bee friends. I know we will have story time, and I think my new teacher is going to read a tail every day. Remember the story about the lion that lost his main?

    I miss you a lot. I hope you can come see me soon.

               Your Friend,

               Max

Spelling Words

Basic Words
1. meet
2. meat
3. week
4. weak
5. mane
6. main
7. tail
8. tale
9. be
10. bee
11. too
12. two

Review Words
13. sea
14. see

1. _____   7. _____

2. _____   8. _____

3. _____   9. _____

4. _____   10. _____

5. _____   11. _____

6. _____   12. _____

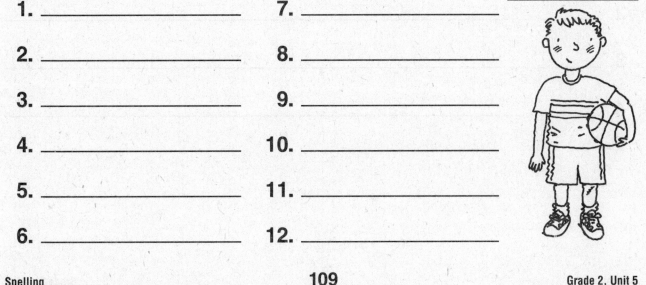

Subject-Verb Agreement

✏️ **Circle the correct verb to go with each subject.**

1. She (play, plays) with me.

2. He (wish, wishes) for good luck.

3. We (throw, throws) a penny in the fountain.

4. They (hope, hopes) her wish comes true.

✏️ **Proofread the paragraph. Circle the four verbs with the wrong endings. Then write each sentence correctly on the lines below.**

Julia is my best friend. She laugh at my jokes.

We watches baseball games. She give me sandwiches.

We shares our toys, too.

1. _____

2. _____

3. _____

4. _____

Evidence

My friend has a new dog.

His dog is <u>smaller</u> than my dog.

His dog is the <u>smallest</u> of all the dogs.

Rewrite the paragraph. Replace each underlined adjective with words from the box that compare.

the fastest of all	longer than my arm
stronger today than yesterday	the highest of all the kites

My friend Bob makes a kite. The tail is <u>long</u>. His

kite looks like a bird. Bob takes the bird kite to the

park. The wind is <u>strong</u>. Many people are flying their

kites. The bird kite is <u>fast</u>. It flies <u>high</u>.

_____

_____

_____

_____

_____

_____

Suffixes *-y, -ly, -ful*

Circle the word that matches each picture. Write the
word and underline the suffix.

1.

wonder   windy   _____

2.

helpful   hopping   _____

3.

snoring   snowy   _____

4.

safely   softer   _____

5.

careful   hurting   _____

Have, Has, and Had

- *Have*, *has*, and *had* are **irregular verbs**.
- Use *have* and *has* to tell about present time.
- Use *had* to tell about something that happened in the past.

Subject	Present	Past
We	have	had
Glenda	has	had
He, She, It	has	had
Ken and Marti	have	had
They	have	had

Jean **has** a new rug now.

Dee and Ben **have** a red rug now.

We **had** a blue rug years ago.

Thinking Question
When does the action take place and who is doing it?

✎ **Circle the word that correctly completes each sentence.**

1. Carrie (have, has) two rugs.

2. Last week she (had, have) three rugs.

3. Now Gus and Lee (had, have) her old rug.

4. Carrie (had, have) no room for her rug.

5. Gus and Lee (has, had) room.

6. They (has, have) a big attic.

Suffixes *-y, -ly, -ful*

Choose a word from the box to complete each sentence.
Then read each sentence aloud with a partner.

Word Bank

-y	-ly	-ful
rusty	quickly	careful
windy	sadly	helpful
	safely	painful

1. Be _____ when you cross the street.

2. _____ put the leash on Rover.

3. The old metal gate is all _____.

4. The boy looked _____ at his broken toy.

5. The splinter in my finger was _____.

6. Put the money _____ in your pocket.

7. Thank you for being so _____.

8. It's so _____ that my hat blew away.

Name _____ Date _____

Suffixes *-ly, -ful*

Sort the Basic Words by the suffixes *-ly* and *-ful*.

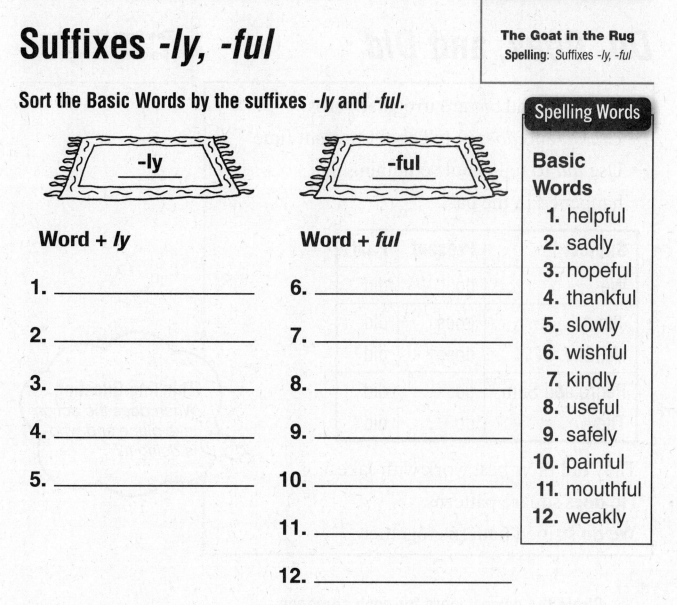

Word + *ly*	Word + *ful*
1. _____	6. _____
2. _____	7. _____
3. _____	8. _____
4. _____	9. _____
5. _____	10. _____
	11. _____
	12. _____

Spelling Words

Basic Words
1. helpful
2. sadly
3. hopeful
4. thankful
5. slowly
6. wishful
7. kindly
8. useful
9. safely
10. painful
11. mouthful
12. weakly

Underline the suffix in each Basic Word.

Do, Does, and Did

- *Do*, *does*, and *did* are **irregular verbs**.
- Use *do* and *does* to tell about present time.
- Use *did* to tell about something that happened in the past.

Subject	Present	Past
We	do	did
Janet	does	did
He, She, It	does	did
Pedro and Sam	do	did
They	do	did

They **did** their best work with Jake.

He **does** square patterns.

We **do** striped patterns together.

Thinking Question
When does the action take place and who is doing it?

✏️ **Circle the correct word for each sentence.**

1. Last week they (do, did) some patterns with Jake.

2. Jake (do, does) great patterns.

3. Yesterday, he (do, did) squares and triangles.

4. Now we (do, does) circles together.

5. He (do, does) his own pattern.

Focus Trait: Elaboration
Synonyms

The Goat in the Rug
Writing: Informative/Explanatory
Writing

Writer's Words	Students' Own Words with Synonyms
You can <u>make</u> wool <u>beautiful</u> colors by <u>soaking</u> it in <u>dye</u>.	You can <u>turn</u> wool <u>pretty</u> colors by <u>dipping</u> it in <u>coloring</u>.

Read the words a writer wrote. Then rewrite the sentence in your own words, using synonyms.

Writer's Words	Your Own Words with Synonyms
1. You can <u>spin</u> wool into <u>threads</u> of yarn.	You can _____ wool into _____ of yarn.
2. A loom can be <u>built</u> using four <u>poles</u>.	A loom can be _____ using four _____.
3. You <u>start</u> weaving at the <u>bottom</u> of the loom.	You _____ weaving at the _____ of the loom.

Syllables *-tion, -ture*

Read the two words in each item below. Think about how the two words are alike. Then write the missing *-tion* or *-ture* word from the Word Bank that fits with each pair of words.

Word Bank

-tion	**-ture**
lotion	creature
vacation	picture
fraction	capture
nation	nature

1. trip, travel, _____

2. animal, beast, _____

3. piece, part of, _____

4. grab, catch, _____

5. a drawing, a painting, a _____

6. weather, plants, _____

7. city, state, _____

8. sunblock, hand cream, _____

Reader's Guide

The Goat in the Rug

Draw and Label a Picture

This story tells how a Navajo woman uses her goat's wool to weave a beautiful rug. Read and answer the questions about the story.

Read pages 281–282. What does Glenmae do first?

_____

Read page 284. What does Glenmae do in this part of the story?

_____

Read page 285. What does Glenmae do with Geraldine's wool now?

_____

Read pages 286–289. What else does Glenmae do?

_____

Read pages 292–294. What does Glenmae do last?

_____

In this story, Glenmae uses many tools. Find four tools in the story. Write and draw them in the order they are used. Write a sentence telling what Glenmae does with each tool.

The tool Glenmae uses first is the _____
She uses the scissors to _____
_____

The tool Glenmae uses second is the _____
She uses the tub to _____
_____

The tool Glenmae uses third is the _____
She uses the comb to _____
_____

The tool Glenmae uses fourth is the _____
She uses the spindle to _____
_____

Suffixes *-ly, -ful*

Write the Spelling Word that matches each meaning.

1. In a slow way   _____

2. Wishing for something   _____

3. In a way with no energy   _____

4. Having hope   _____

5. In a sad way   _____

6. Giving help   _____

7. Being kind   _____

8. Being put to use   _____

9. In a way that won't hurt you   _____

10. A lot of food in your mouth   _____

11. Full of thanks   _____

12. Full of pain   _____

Spelling Words

**Basic
Words**
1. helpful
2. sadly
3. hopeful
4. thankful
5. slowly
6. wishful
7. kindly
8. useful
9. safely
10. painful
11. mouthful
12. weakly

Irregular Verbs

Circle the verb that correctly completes each sentence.

1. Last week the goat and lamb (have, had) long hair.

2. Yesterday they (have, had) a hair cut.

3. The lamb (has, have) short hair now.

4. The goat (has, have) short hair, too.

5. Now we (have, had) wool to make a rug.

Write the correct verb to finish each sentence.

6. Gerry _____ something fun.
(do   does)

7. Tonya and Raj _____ a dance on the rug.
(do   does)

8. They _____ their favorite dance yesterday.
(do   did)

9. Gerry _____ his best when he jumped.
(did   do)

10. He _____ his best right now.
(do   does)

Compound Words

Draw a line between the words that make up each compound word in the Word Bank. Use what you know about the shorter words to predict the compound word's meaning. Complete each sentence by writing the compound word whose meaning fits the best.

Word Bank

doormat	rosebush	backyard	doorbell
mailbox	sandbox	sidewalk	trashcan

1. The children sat in the _____ and

filled the pails with sand.

2. "Let's go to the _____ ," said Robert.

"I want to climb the oak tree."

3. Mr. Hendricks wiped his feet on the _____

before going into the house.

4. We thought we heard the _____ ring,

but nobody was there.

5. Larry found two letters in his _____ .

6. The _____ is full. I better empty it.

7. "Ouch," said Theresa. "This _____

has a lot of thorns.

8. Sometimes Steve skateboards on the _____.

Proofread for Spelling

The Goat in the Rug
Spelling: Suffixes *-ly, -ful*

Proofread Bert's story. Circle the eight misspelled words. Then write the correct spellings on the lines below.

Last week we went to visit my grandpa's farm. I couldn't wait, but my dad kept driving slowlee! When we finally arrived, Grandpa took me to the barn.

In the corner of a pen, I saw a goat breathing weakely. Saddly, Grandpa said it was sick. The vet gave the goat some pills. The goat ate them with a mothful of corn. Grandpa was hopful that the goat would get well. I stayed safly out of the pen. It would be paynful if the goat kicked me.

After dinner, Grandpa and I went to check on the goat. It was running around in its pen! Grandpa and I were happy and tankful that the goat was feeling better.

Spelling Words

Basic Words
1. helpful
2. sadly
3. hopeful
4. thankful
5. slowly
6. wishful
7. kindly
8. useful
9. safely
10. painful
11. mouthful
12. weakly

1. _____   5. _____

2. _____   8. _____

3. _____   7. _____

4. _____   8. _____

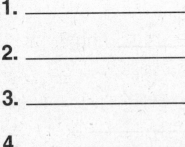

Forms of the Verb *be*

✏️ Circle the correct form of the verb *be*. Then rewrite the sentence on the line below.

1. The women (are, is) weavers.

_____

2. The wool (is, were) soft.

_____

3. The rugs (were, was) pretty.

_____

4. We (are, is) interested in rugs.

_____

5. I (am, is) in a rug store.

_____

6. It (is, are) a new rug.

_____

7. That (are, is) the one I want.

_____

8. The other rugs (was, were) too large.

_____

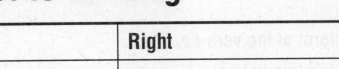
Connect to Writing

Wrong	Right
We <u>has</u> a new rug.	We <u>have</u> a new rug.

Read the paragraphs. Find six verb mistakes. Then rewrite each sentence. Make sure each verb matches the subject in the sentence.

Sue Makes Rugs

Sue have a loom now. She likes to weave rugs. We has a rug from her now. I watch Sue work. She do a lot to get ready to weave.

Last week, Sue needed wool. Yesterday, Sue do a trade with the owner of the wool store. Now the owner have a rug, too. Now Sue have enough wool for many rugs!

_____

_____

_____

_____

_____

_____

_____

Name _____ Date _____

Prefixes

Make words with prefixes. Read the base word.
Then add the prefix at the top of the column and
write the new word.

	un-	re-
1. lock	_____	_____
2. tie	_____	_____
3. pin	_____	_____
4. fold	_____	_____
5. pack	_____	_____

Complete each sentence. Add a prefix from the box to the base
word at the end of the sentence. Write the new word on the line.

over-	pre-	mis-

6. Set an alarm clock so you do not

_____. **sleep**

7. Before the real test, we will have a

_____. **test**

8. Be careful not to _____

any words. **spell**

Irregular Action Verbs

- *Run, come, sit, hide,* and *tell* are **irregular verbs**. You do not add an *-ed* ending to these verbs to tell about the past.

Thinking Question
Is the action happening now or did it happen in the past?

Happening Now	Happened in the Past
The ducks **come** to the pond.	The ducks **came** to the pond.
The chipmunks **run** away.	The chipmunks **ran** away.
The pigs **sit** in the mud.	The pigs **sat** in the mud.
The children **hide** in the field.	The children **hid** in the field.
The parents **tell** a story.	The parents **told** a story.

Read and circle the word that tells when the action happens. Write each sentence using the correct verb.

1. The cows (come, came) from the fields.   **now**

_____

2. The children (run, ran) down the path.   **now**

_____

3. They (sit, sat) in the field.   **past**

_____

4. They all (hide, hid) in the dark.   **past**

_____

Prefixes

Read each word. Then write the prefix and base word
on the lines.

1. unsafe _____   _____

2. recheck _____   _____

3. retell _____   _____

4. overeat _____   _____

5. unwise _____   _____

6. repaint _____   _____

Add the prefix *re-, mis-,* or *pre-* to the base word at the end of
each sentence. Write the new word on the line to complete
the sentence.

7. I _____ the oven before

I bake. **heat**

8. I listen carefully so I won't

_____. **understand**

9. I will study again and _____

the test. **take**

Prefixes *re-* and *un-*

Sort the Basic Words by the prefixes *re-* and *un-*.
Underline the prefix in each word.

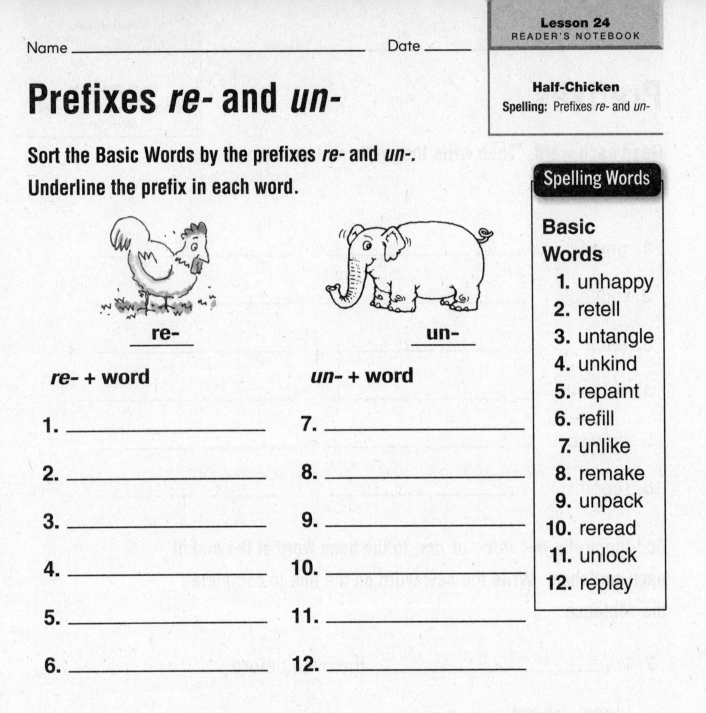

re- _____   **un-** _____

re- + word   **un- + word**

1. _____   7. _____

2. _____   8. _____

3. _____   9. _____

4. _____   10. _____

5. _____   11. _____

6. _____   12. _____

Spelling Words

Basic Words
1. unhappy
2. retell
3. untangle
4. unkind
5. repaint
6. refill
7. unlike
8. remake
9. unpack
10. reread
11. unlock
12. replay

Name _____ Date _____

Lesson 24
READER'S NOTEBOOK

See, Saw and Go, Went

- *See* and *go* are **irregular verbs**. Do not add an *-ed* ending to these verbs to tell about the past.
- *See* tells about an action happening now. *Saw* tells about an action in the past.
- *Go* tells about an action happening now. *Went* tells about an action in the past.

Thinking Question
Is the action happening now or did it happen in the past?

Happening Now	Happened in the Past
The squirrels **go** up a tree.	The squirrels **went** up a tree.
The squirrels **see** their food.	The squirrels **saw** their food.

Read the word that tells when the action happens. Write each sentence using the correct verb.

1. The chicks (see, saw) their mother.   **now**

_____

2. The chicks (go, went) with their mother.   **now**

_____

3. All of the chickens (see, saw) the chicks.   **past**

_____

4. The chickens (go, went) quickly to their nests.   **past**

_____

Focus Trait: Evidence
Exact Details

Sentence	Sentence with Exact Details
Animals live on this ranch.	**Horses, pigs, chickens, and cows** live on this ranch.

A. Read each sentence. Add exact details to make each sentence clearer and more interesting.

Sentence	Sentence with Exact Details
1. The hen ate.	The _____ hen _____
2. The chicks gathered around their mother.	The _____ chicks gathered around their mother _____

B. Read each sentence. Look at the picture on pages 320–321 of *Half-Chicken*. Add exact details to make each sentence clearer.

Sentence	Sentence with Exact Details
3. Everyone came to see.	
4. Plants grew in the field.	

Silent Consonants

Write a word from the sentence to answer the question.

1. Would you **kneel** or **knit** a hat? _____

2. Would you **crumb** or **climb** a hill? _____

3. Would you **knob** or **knock** on a door? _____

4. Could you bend a **wrong** or a **wrist**? _____

5. Would you tie a **knot** or a **knife**? _____

6. Is a **gnat** or a **gnu** very small? _____

7. Would a **comb** or a **lamb** eat grass? _____

8. Would you **wrench** or **wrap** a gift? _____

Use words from above to write two new sentences.

9. _____

10. _____

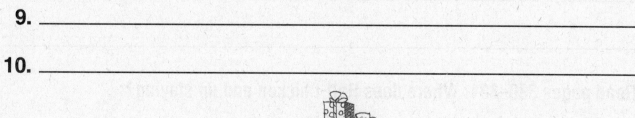

Reader's Guide

Half-Chicken

Draw and Label a Picture

This story tells about a very special chicken and his
trip to Mexico City. Reread pages from the story and
write what happened at each part of the trip.

Read page 321. Why does Half-Chicken decide to go on a trip?

_____

_____

Read pages 323–324. Who does he help along the way?

_____

_____

Read pages 327–329. What happens in the viceroy's court?

_____

_____

Read pages 330–331. Where does Half-Chicken end up staying?

_____

_____

Half-Chicken wants to send a postcard to his family. Draw a picture on the front. Tell the story of Half-Chicken's adventure on the back.

Front

Back

Dear Family,
_____
_____
_____
_____
_____
_____
_____

Mrs. Chicken and Family

The Ranch

Countryside, Mexico City

Prefixes *re-* and *un-*

Write the Basic Word that matches each meaning.

1. fill again _____

2. tell again _____

3. read again _____

4. play again _____

5. make again _____

6. paint again _____

7. not happy _____

8. not like _____

9. not kind _____

10. undo a lock _____

Spelling Words

Basic Words
1. unhappy
2. retell
3. untangle
4. unkind
5. repaint
6. refill
7. unlike
8. remake
9. unpack
10. reread
11. unlock
12. replay

Irregular Action Verbs

Read the word that tells when the action happens.
Then write each sentence using the correct verb.

1. The horses (hide, hid) with their babies.   **now**

_____

2. The colts (come, came) to the water.   **now**

_____

3. The animals (run, ran) for a drink.   **past**

_____

4. The boys (see, saw) the horses.   **past**

_____

5. The girls (go, went) to the barn.   **past**

_____

6. The dogs (sit, sat) with the girls.   **now**

_____

7. The girls (tell, told) the boys where to go.   **past**

_____

Antonyms

Circle the two words that are antonyms in each sentence.

1. James put his wet shirt in the sun so it would get dry.

2. Cindy put the soft pillow on the hard chair.

3. Nathan filled a tall glass with water and sat down to do his short paper.

4. Amy used her strong arms to pull down the weak and broken branches of the tree.

Circle the two words in each group that are antonyms.

5.   swift   steady   slow

6.   high   full   empty

7.   cold   hot   cloudy

8.   sunny   hilly   cloudy

9.   before   over   under

10. smooth   bumpy   brush

Proofread for Spelling

Proofread the newspaper article. Circle the eight misspelled words. Then write the correct spellings on the lines below.

Spelling Words

Basic Words

1. unhappy
2. retell
3. untangle
4. unkind
5. repaint
6. refill
7. unlike
8. remake
9. unpack
10. reread
11. unlock
12. replay

New at the Ranch

The Wild Bill Ranch is getting a new prize bull named Ollie.

This morning, ranch hands arrived to unpak a huge crate. Out came a very unhapi bull.

"It might seem unkined to put Ollie in a crate," said the rancher. "But it was the best way to keep him safe. Once we unlok the crate and untanglel Ollie from his blanket, he will soon forget about it. Ollie's new space is unlik the small pen he once called home."

Watch tonight's news to see a repla of Ollie's arrival. You can buy the book that reteels Ollie's story.

1. _____   5. _____

2. _____   6. _____

3. _____   7. _____

4. _____   8. _____

Commas in Dates and Places

✎ Read each sentence. Rewrite each date or place. Put the comma in the correct place.

1. We visited Mexico on June 17 2011.

_____

2. I came from Atlanta Georgia.

_____

3. We saw horses on June 20 2011.

_____

4. Later, I visited Chicago Illinois.

_____

5. The baby elephant was born on April, 2 2012.

_____

6. I heard the story in Miami Florida.

_____

7. I took a plane to Los Angeles California.

_____

8. I saw ten chicks on May 1 2012.

_____

Connect to Writing Using Exact Verbs

Without Exact Verb	With Exact Verb
The lions <u>move</u> quickly	The lions <u>dash</u> quickly.

✏ **Replace each underlined word with an exact word from the box. Write the new sentences. Underline the exact words.**

race	hurt	watched	hid	squawks

1. Yesterday, I <u>saw</u> a fox.

   _____

2. I saw the fox <u>move</u> past our barn.

   _____

3. The chickens made many <u>noises</u>.

   _____

4. Finally, they <u>sat</u> in their nests.

   _____

5. They thought the fox would <u>bother</u> them.

   _____

Lesson 25
READER'S NOTEBOOK

From Seed to Plant
Phonics: Words with *au, aw,*
al, o, a

Words with *au, aw, al, o, a*

Complete the puzzle with words that have the vowel sound you hear in *saw*.

Read each clue. Then choose a word from the box.

Word Bank

toss	straw	tall	paw	salt
frost	pause	lost	soft	lawn

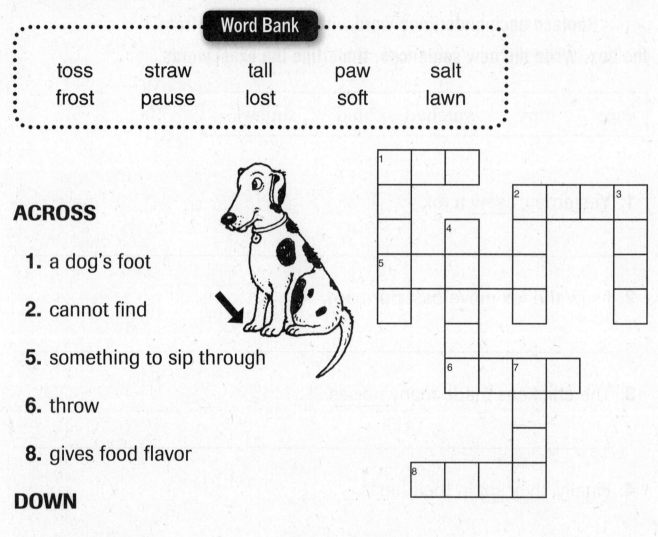

ACROSS

1. a dog's foot

2. cannot find

5. something to sip through

6. throw

8. gives food flavor

DOWN

1. a quick stop

2. grass

3. not short

4. icy coating

7. not hard

Name _____ Date _____

Say, Said and Eat, Ate

From Seed to Plant
Grammar: More Irregular Action Verbs

- The verbs *say* and *eat* are **irregular verbs**.
- *Say* tells about an action happening now. *Said* tells about an action in the past.
- *Eat* tells about an action happening now. *Ate* tells about an action in the past.

Happening Now	Happened in the Past
The rabbits **say** they are hungry now.	Then the rabbits **said** they were hungry.
Today, the rabbits **eat** lunch.	The rabbits **ate** lunch yesterday.

Thinking Question
Is the action happening now or did it happen in the past?

Read each sentence. Underline the correct verb. Then rewrite each sentence using the correct verb.

1. Yesterday, the rabbits (eat, ate) carrots. **past**

_____

2. They (say, said) that they were still hungry. **past**

_____

3. Today, they (eat, ate) tomatoes. **now**

_____

4. Now the rabbits (say, said) they are still hungry. **now**

_____

Grammar
© Houghton Mifflin Harcourt Publishing Company. All rights reserved.
143
Grade 2, Unit 5

Words with *au*, *aw*, *al*, *o*, *a*

In each row, circle the words that have the /aw/ sound
as in *saw*.

1. flaw	hog	some	ball	soft

2. talk	cold	drawn	hang	launch

3. smoke	salt	small	faucet	off

4. toss	awful	cane	pale	water

5. mall	chalk	jaw	autumn	yawn

Circle the word that completes the sentence and write
it on the line.

6. Paul and I went for a _____.

    frost   walk

7. A _____ sat on a high branch.

    haul   hawk

8. I saw its sharp _____.

    claws   clogs

Words with *aw, al, o*

Sort the Spelling Words by the /aw/ sound spelled
al, aw, and *o.*

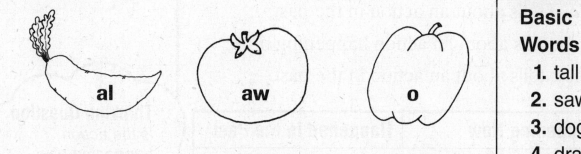

al   aw   o

al words	*aw* words	*o* words
1. _____	8. _____	12. _____
2. _____	9. _____	13. _____
3. _____	10. _____	14. _____
4. _____	11. _____	
5. _____		
6. _____		
7. _____		

Spelling Words

Basic Words
1. tall
2. saw
3. dog
4. draw
5. call
6. fall
7. soft
8. paw
9. ball
10. yawn
11. log
12. small

Review Words
13. all
14. walk

Give, Gave and Take, Took

- The verbs *give* and *take* are **irregular verbs**.
- *Give* tells about an action happening now.
  Gave tells about an action in the past.
- *Take* tells about an action happening now.
  Took tells about an action in the past.

Happening Now	Happened in the Past
They **give** the gardener seeds now.	Last fall they **gave** the gardener seeds.
They **take** the vegetables home now.	They **took** the vegetables home yesterday.

Thinking Question
Is the action happening now or did it happen in the past?

Read each sentence. Underline the correct verb. Then rewrite each sentence using the correct verb.

1. Last year, the children (give, gave) me seeds.   **past**

_____

2. I (take, took) the seeds to my garden last spring.   **past**

_____

3. All that summer, I (give, gave) the plants water.   **past**

_____

4. Now I (take, took) vegetables from my garden.   **now**

_____

Name _____ Date _____

Lesson 25
READER'S NOTEBOOK

From Seed to Plant
Writing: Informative Writing

Focus Trait: Elaboration Using Your Own Words

Original Sentences	Writer's Own Words
Plants such as pumpkins, zucchini, yellow squash, and sunflowers grow very big. Their seeds need to be planted far apart to give them room to grow.	Some plants are very big. They need extra room to grow. Be careful not to plant their seeds close together.

Read each original sentence or set of sentences. Paraphrase each by using different words to give the same information.

Original Sentences	Your Own Words
1. Sometimes it is hard to find potatoes in a garden because they grow underground.	
2. Rabbits eat only plants. They use their long ears to listen for animals that might eat them.	
3. Bees and butterflies carry pollen from flower to flower.	
4. Some scientists believe the tomato first came from Mexico.	
5. Thousands of types of apples exist.	

Writing
147
Grade 2, Unit 5

Cumulative Review

Read each question. Make a word that answers each question by choosing a word from the box and adding the suffix *-y, -ly,* or *-ful* to it.

Word Bank

hand	rock	neat
skill	bump	

Which word describes . . .

1. a place with rocks? _____

2. someone with a skill? _____

3. working in a neat way? _____

4. an amount held in a hand? _____

5. a road with bumps? _____

Add *-y, -ly,* or *-ful* to the word in bold print so that the sentence makes sense.

6. The kitten is very **play**. _____

7. She walks **soft** across the tile. _____

8. She gets **sleep** in the daytime. _____

Reader's Guide

From Seed to Plant

Scientist's Notebook

Be a scientist! Study growing plants to see what happens. Take notes and make sketches in your research log.

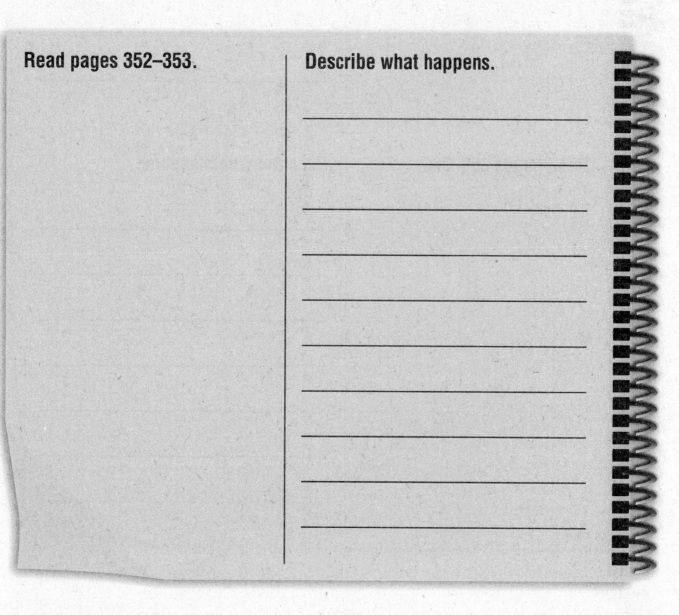

Read pages 352–353.

Describe what happens.

_____

_____

_____

_____

_____

_____

_____

_____

_____

Read pages 354–356.

Describe what happens.

_____

_____

_____

_____

_____

_____

Read pages 359–360.

Describe what happens.

_____

_____

_____

_____

_____

_____

_____

Lesson 25
READER'S NOTEBOOK

From Seed to Plant
Spelling: Words with *aw, al, o*

Words with *aw, al, o*

Write the Spelling Word that belongs in each group.

Spelling Words

Basic Words

1. tall
2. saw
3. dog
4. draw
5. call
6. fall
7. soft
8. paw
9. ball
10. yawn
11. log
12. small

Review Words

13. all
14. walk

1. wood, tree, _____

2. foot, hoof, _____

3. cat, bird, _____

4. heard, touched, _____

5. paint, sketch, _____

6. bat, glove, _____

7. summer, winter, _____

8. shout, yell, _____

9. sleep, snore, _____

Write the Spelling Word that is the opposite of the given word.

10. hard _____

11. short _____

12. none _____

13. run _____

14. large _____

More Irregular Action Verbs

✎ Read each sentence. Use the clue and underline the correct verb. Then rewrite each sentence using the correct verb that tells about now or the past.

1. The farmers (say, said) they planted corn.   **past**

_____

2. Today, the children (eat, ate) a lot of corn.   **now**

_____

3. The farmers (say, said) they can bring more corn.   **now**

_____

4. We (give, gave) vegetables to our friends.   **past**

_____

5. They (give, gave) us fruit from their trees.   **now**

_____

6. We (take, took) two apples from the basket.   **now**

_____

Using Context

Use clues in the sentence to find the meaning of the underlined word. Then find the word's meaning in the box. Write the definition on the line.

Word Bank

something that helps plants grow   move quickly
take small bites   speak with anger
someone who lives nearby   lucky

1. I like to <u>nibble</u> the carrot. I eat it like a bunny.

_____

2. Lisa is very late. She has to <u>rush</u> to catch the school

bus. _____

3. Please don't <u>scold</u> me. I did not mean to drop the

cup. _____

4. Jake is our <u>neighbor</u>. He walks to my house to play.

_____

5. Dad uses <u>fertilizer</u> in the garden. He wants the plants

to be healthy. _____

6. My sister has the flu. I feel very <u>fortunate</u> that I

didn't catch it. _____

Proofread for Spelling

Proofread this journal entry. Circle the eight misspelled words. Then write the correct spellings on the lines below.

April 10, 2010

    I think spring is here. Today I sow a robin. I have not seen one since last fal. I like spring because I spend more time outside.

    I like to plant seeds in the sawft mud of Mom's flower garden. Then I drow pictures of the flowers on smoll cards and place the signs at the head of each row.

    My dog Max likes to help, but just one paw can smash my plants. Mom will call him away to chase his ball. Sometimes Max will just sit near me and yown in the sun.

    Soon my plants will grow toll. Then I will sit on a lawg and smell my flowers.

Spelling Words
Basic Words
1. tall
2. saw
3. dog
4. draw
5. call
6. fall
7. soft
8. paw
9. ball
10. yawn
11. log
12. small

1. _____ 5. _____

2. _____ 6. _____

3. _____ 7. _____

4. _____ 8. _____

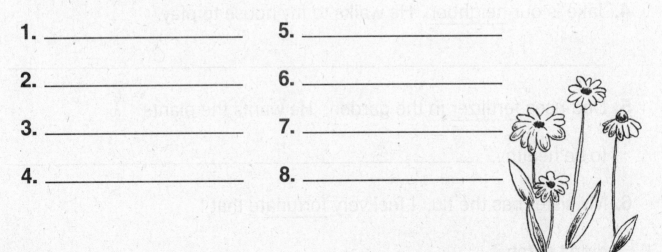

Commas in a Series

Draw a line under each correct sentence.

1. Mom's garden has tomatoes, peppers and squash.

    Mom's garden has tomatoes, peppers, and squash.

2. She planted on Sunday, Monday, and Tuesday.

    She planted, on Sunday Monday and Tuesday.

3. We helped her dig plant, and water.

    We helped her dig, plant, and water.

4. I planted the carrots celery and eggplant.

    I planted the carrots, celery, and eggplant.

5. We saw, bees, birds and butterflies on the plants.

    We saw bees, birds, and butterflies on the plants.

6. We will have vegetables in June, July, and August.

    We will have vegetables in, June July and, August.

Connect to Writing

Incorrect

Last week she **gives** me a bag of carrots.

I **taked** the carrots home.

Correct

Last week she **gave** me a bag of carrots.

I **took** the carrots home.

Read this story about last summer. Write the paragraph correctly. Change each underlined verb to tell about the past.

My Summer Garden

Last year, I grew a garden. I <u>take</u> seeds and put them in the ground. I <u>gived</u> them water. Mom and Dad <u>say</u> we could pick the vegetables when they grew. Soon, the garden grew. I <u>give</u> eggplant to Mom. I <u>take</u> carrots for myself. We <u>eat</u> it all. Yum!

_____

_____

_____

_____

_____

Words with *oo, ew, ue, ou*

The Mysterious Tadpole
Phonics: Words with *oo, ew, ue, ou*

Put these letters together to write words with the vowel sound you hear in *zoo*.

1. m + oo + n _____

2. s + ou + p _____

3. c + h + ew _____

4. b + l + ue _____

5. p + oo + l _____

Now use the words you wrote above to complete the sentences below.

6. Did you see the _____ and the stars last night?

7. We swim in the _____.

8. I ate a bowl of hot _____.

9. The sun is shining in the _____ sky.

10. Our puppy likes to _____ on socks.

Contractions with *not*

- A **contraction** is a short way of writing two words.
- An **apostrophe (')** shows where letters were left out.

Two Words	Contraction
do not	**don't**
does not	**doesn't**
is not	**isn't**
cannot	**can't**

Thinking Question
Which two words are being put together to make a contraction?

✏️ **Write contractions for the underlined words.**

1. I <u>do not</u> believe my eyes! _____

2. Your pet <u>is not</u> friendly. _____

3. I <u>cannot</u> believe your pig can fly. _____

4. Your pig <u>does not</u> have wings. _____

5. I <u>do not</u> know how it can fly! _____

6. Our art teacher <u>does not</u> come on Tuesdays.

_____

Words with *oo, ew, ue, ou*

Answer each pair of clues using the words below the clues.

1. Something that helps solve a mystery _____

The people who work on a ship _____

crew   **clue**

2. To move quickly _____

A place to see animals _____

zoom   **zoo**

3. Many people together _____

Got bigger _____

group   **grew**

4. Lift or push someone from below _____

In a little while _____

soon   **boost**

5. Moved by using wings _____

Not many _____

flew   **few**

Name _____ Date _____

Lesson 26
READER'S NOTEBOOK

The Mysterious Tadpole
Spelling: Words with *oo*
(ew, oo, ou)

Words with *oo* (ew, oo, ou)

Sort the words by the spelling for the vowel sound in *moon*.

With *oo*   **With *ew***   **With *ou***

1. _____   9. _____   14. _____

2. _____   10. _____

3. _____   11. _____

4. _____   12. _____

5. _____   13. _____

6. _____

7. _____

8. _____

Underline the letters in each word that make the vowel sound in *moon*.

Spelling Words
Basic Words
1. root
2. crew
3. spoon
4. few
5. bloom
6. grew
7. room
8. you
9. stew
10. boost
11. scoop
12. flew
Review Words
13. zoo
14. noon

Contractions with Pronouns

The Mysterious Tadpole
Grammar: Contractions

- A **contraction** is a word made by putting two words together.
- An **apostrophe** replaces the letter or letters that were left out.
- Many contractions are made by joining a **pronoun** and a **verb**.

Two Words	Contraction
I am	I'm
You will	You'll
She will	She'll
We are	We're
They are	They're
She is	She's
It is	It's

Thinking Question
Which two words are being put together to make a contraction?

Write contractions for the underlined words.

1. <u>I am</u> surprised to see a pink tadpole. _____

2. <u>They are</u> supposed to be brown. _____

3. <u>It is</u> a funny looking creature. _____

4. <u>We are</u> not sure why it is so big. _____

5. <u>You will</u> wonder about this strange pet. _____

Focus Trait: Elaboration
Sense Words and Details

The Mysterious Tadpole
Writing: Opinion Writing

Without Sense Words and Details	With Sense Words and Details
Louis saw a tadpole.	Louis saw a **huge spotted** tadpole.

A. Complete each sentence, using sense words and details.

   Use the hint in ( ) to help you.

Without Sense Words and Details	With Sense Words and Details
1. Louis touched Alphonse's skin. (touch)	Louis touched Alphonse's _____ skin.
2. Louis smelled the water. (smell)	Louis smelled the _____ water.

B. Read each weak sentence. Rewrite each sentence.

   Add sense words and details.

Pair/Share Work with a partner to brainstorm powerful words.

Weak Language	Powerful Language
3. Alphonse ate a snack.	
4. Louis heard a sound.	

Cumulative Review

Add the suffix *-y*, *-ly*, or *-ful* to each word. Write the word on the line and read each completed sentence.

1. **rain**: I painted my bedroom one

   _____ day.

2. **slow**: I painted _____.

3. **care**: I was _____ not to spill.

4. **hope**: Mom was _____ that I

   would finish by noon.

5. **quick**: I tried painting _____.

6. **mess**: It was _____.

Add the prefix to each base word. Then write the new word on the line.

7. re + paint = _____

8. un + cover = _____

9. over + look = _____

10. pre + mix = _____

11. mis + match = _____

Reader's Guide

The Mysterious Tadpole

Write a Letter

Hi. I'm Louis. My uncle gave me a pet. Use the text and illustrations to help me write letters about my amazing pet!

Read pages 386–387. Then write a letter from Louis to Uncle McAllister.

Dear Uncle McAllister,

_____

_____

_____

Love, Louis

Read pages 388 and 391. Then write another letter to Uncle McAllister. What happened since your last letter?

Dear Uncle McAllister,

_____

_____

Love, Louis

Read pages 397–399. Write another letter from Louis to Uncle McAllister. Let him know what happened on these pages.

Dear Uncle McAllister,

_____

_____

_____

_____

Love, Louis

Read pages 400–402. What happens in this part of the story? Use what you read to write another letter from Louis to Uncle McAllister.

Dear Uncle McAllister,

_____

_____

_____

_____

Love, Louis

Words with *oo (ew, oo, ou)*

The Mysterious Tadpole
Spelling: Words with *oo*
(*ew, oo, ou*)

Write the Spelling Word that matches each meaning.

1. not many _____

2. got bigger _____

3. animal park _____

4. raise _____

5. midday _____

6. pick up _____

Write the Basic Word that belongs in each group.

7. glided, floated, _____

8. team, helpers, _____

9. knife, fork, _____

10. chowder, chili, _____

11. kitchen, den, _____

12. flower, open, _____

13. tree, trunk, _____

14. me, us, _____

Spelling Words

Basic Words

1. root
2. crew
3. spoon
4. few
5. bloom
6. grew
7. room
8. you
9. stew
10. boost
11. scoop
12. flew

Review Words

13. zoo
14. noon

Contractions

Write the contraction for each underlined word or words.

1. Tina knows that cats <u>do not</u> talk. _____

2. She <u>is not</u> sure why her cat can sing. _____

3. Tina <u>cannot</u> tell people about the cat. _____

4. She <u>does not</u> think anyone will believe her.

_____

Write each sentence. Write a contraction in place of the underlined words.

5. <u>We are</u> tadpoles in a pond.

_____

6. <u>They are</u> afraid of us.

_____

7. <u>You will</u> see that I am small.

_____

8. But <u>I am</u> going to be ten feet tall!

_____

Name _____ Date _____

Lesson 26
READER'S NOTEBOOK

The Mysterious Tadpole
Vocabulary Strategies:
Multiple-Meaning Words

Multiple-Meaning Words

Read the words and their definitions. Decide which
meaning fits the underlined word in each sentence
below. Write the correct definition on the line.

fly	**1.** a small insect with wings
	2. to move through the air like a bird or insect
line	**1.** a number of people or things in a row
	2. a long piece of string or wire used for fishing
upset	**1.** unhappy or disappointed about something
	2. to turn, tip, or knock something over

1. Ed used a worm as bait on his fishing <u>line</u>.

_____

2. Sasha got <u>upset</u> when she heard the bad news.

_____

3. The kids waited in <u>line</u> to get a drink of water.

_____

4. An eagle can <u>fly</u> for many miles.

_____

5. The <u>fly</u> was buzzing around the picnic table.

_____

The Mysterious Tadpole
Spelling: Words with *oo*
(*ew, oo, ou*)

Proofread for Spelling

**Proofread the paragraphs. Circle the eight misspelled words.
Then write the correct spellings on the lines below.**

Do yoo have a plant? When I groo up, I had a
plant in my ruem. It was a pretty little tree. It grew
inside a pot. Its rewts were deep.

I fed the plant every month. I gave it a fou
scups of plant food. In the summer, I would bewst it
up to the window so it could get more sun. Once a year,
it grew beautiful red bloums.

Spelling Words
1. root
2. crew
3. spoon
4. few
5. bloom
6. grew
7. room
8. you
9. stew
10. boost
11. scoop
12. flew

1. _____   5. _____

2. _____   6. _____

3. _____   7. _____

4. _____   8. _____

**Write these other Spelling Words in ABC order: *crew, spoon,
stew, flew.***

9. _____   11. _____

10. _____   12. _____

Kinds of Adjectives

✏️ **Circle the adjective that best completes the sentence. Use the clue at the end of the sentence.**

1. The tadpoles are (big, brown). (color)

2. There are (forty, long) of them. (how many)

3. They are (tall, slippery). (feel)

4. They are (tiny, angry). (size)

✏️ **Read each pair of sentences. Join the sentences using and between the two adjectives. Write the new sentence.**

5. The ocean water was deep.

The ocean water was cold.

_____

6. The fish were happy.

The fish were surprised.

_____

Connect to Writing

Incorrect	Correct
The mysterious horse <u>is'nt</u> growing.	The mysterious horse <u>isn't</u> growing.
<u>H'es</u> getting smaller!	<u>He's</u> getting smaller!

Read the paragraph. Circle five mistakes with contractions. Copy the story and write the contractions correctly.

The Mysterious Horse

Im' going to tell you a story. I once knew a pony named Lou. He was'nt a big pony. And he did'nt get any bigger, either. One day he started to shrink. H'es still getting smaller today. I think one day hel'l be the smallest horse in the world!

_____

_____

_____

_____

_____

Words with *oo* as in *book*

The Dog That Dug for Dinosaurs
Phonics: Words with *oo*
(book)

Word Bank

cookbook   cook   took
good   cookies   looking

Write a word from the box to complete each sentence. Then read each completed sentence.

1. My father and I like to _____.

2. Last Saturday I was _____

for something to do.

3. "Let's bake oatmeal _____,"

said Dad.

4. We followed all the steps in the _____.

5. Mom _____ one of our treats.

6. She agreed that they tasted _____.

Write two rhyming words for each word below.

      cook   **good**

_____   _____

_____   _____

Lesson 27
READER'S NOTEBOOK

The Dog That Dug for Dinosaurs
Grammar: What Is an Adverb?

Adverbs That Tell How

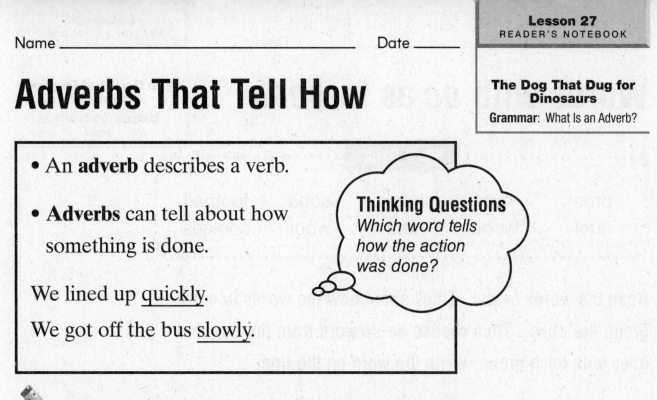

- An **adverb** describes a verb.

- **Adverbs** can tell about how something is done.

We lined up <u>quickly</u>.

We got off the bus <u>slowly</u>.

Thinking Questions
Which word tells how the action was done?

Read each sentence. Think about the action. Then underline the adverb that tells how the action was done.

1. The bus driver spoke loudly.

2. He carefully called each name.

3. She raised her hand shyly.

4. He nicely helped her climb the steps.

5. They got to the museum quickly.

6. Quietly, the children asked questions.

7. They looked at the dinosaurs together.

8. Then they talked softly.

Words with *oo* as in *book*

Word Bank

brook	hoof	hook	good	football
look	wood	foot	woof	cookies

Read the words below. Think about how the words in each group are alike. Then choose an *oo* word from the box that goes with each group. Write the word on the line.

1. hand, eye, _____

2. kickball, baseball, _____

3. nice, fine, _____

4. mane, tail, _____

5. moo, chirp, _____

6. creek, stream, _____

7. pies, cakes, _____

8. see, peek, _____

9. brick, glass, _____

10. bait, pole, _____

Words with *oo* as in *book*

Sort the Spelling Words by final consonants.

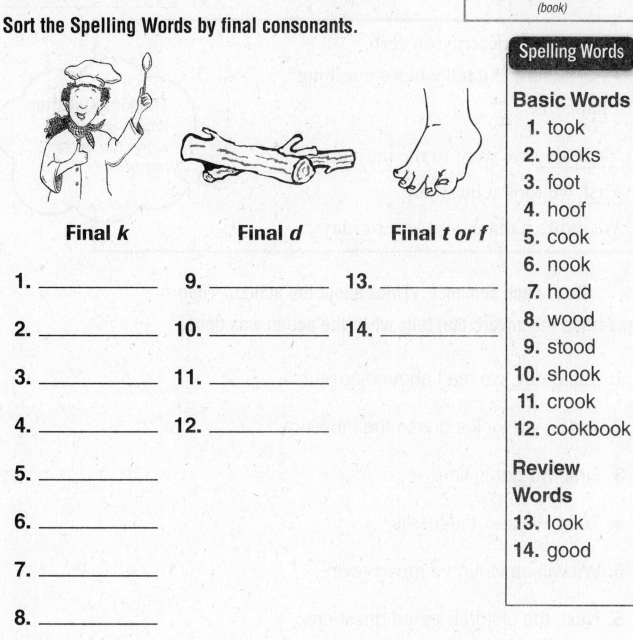

Final *k*	**Final *d***	**Final *t* or *f***
1. _____	9. _____	13. _____
2. _____	10. _____	14. _____
3. _____	11. _____	
4. _____	12. _____	
5. _____		
6. _____		
7. _____		
8. _____		

Spelling Words

Basic Words
1. took
2. books
3. foot
4. hoof
5. cook
6. nook
7. hood
8. wood
9. stood
10. shook
11. crook
12. cookbook

Review Words
13. look
14. good

Adverbs That Tell When

- An **adverb** describes a verb.
- An **adverb** can tell when something happens.

Yesterday, we went to the museum.

First, we took a bus there.

We wrote a thank-you letter today.

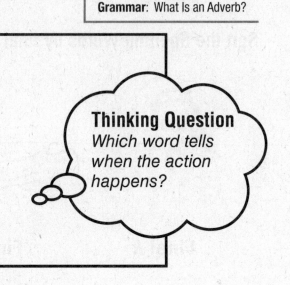

Thinking Question
*Which word tells
when the action
happens?*

✏ **Read each sentence. Think about the action. Then underline the adverb that tells when the action was done.**

1. Yesterday, we read about dinosaurs.

2. Today, we took a bus to the museum.

3. First, we got in line.

4. Then, we saw the fossils.

5. We will be writing a report soon.

6. Next, the children asked questions.

7. They looked at the dinosaurs later.

8. Then, they talked on the bus.

Focus Trait: Organization Introduction and Conclusion

The **introduction sentence** of a book report tells about the book and gives an opinion about the book.

Sentences that give **reasons** tell facts to support the opinion.

The **conclusion sentence** sums up the information and tells the opinion in a different way.

Label the introduction sentence, the sentences that give reasons, and the conclusion sentence.

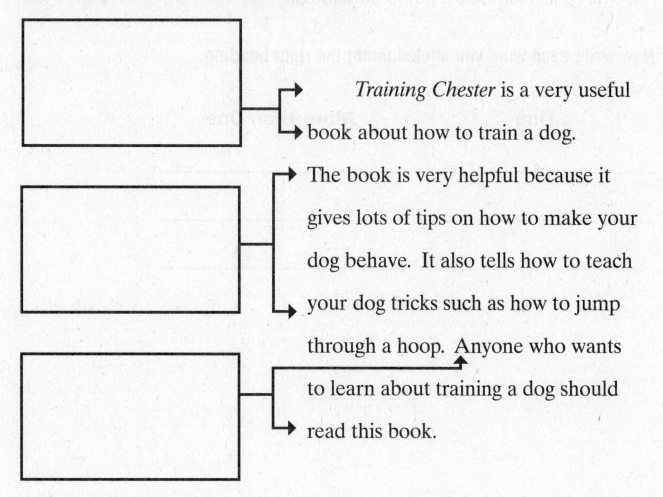

Training Chester is a very useful book about how to train a dog.

The book is very helpful because it gives lots of tips on how to make your dog behave. It also tells how to teach your dog tricks such as how to jump through a hoop. Anyone who wants to learn about training a dog should read this book.

Possessive Nouns

Read the sentences. Draw a circle around each word that shows who or what owns something.

1. The bike's tire is flat.

2. We laughed at the seals' tricks.

3. The ladies' club has a meeting today.

4. The little rabbit's tail is white and fluffy.

5. The book's pages are torn.

6. The girls' team has a game on Thursday.

Now write each word you circled under the right heading.

One	More Than One
_____	_____
_____	_____
_____	_____

Name _____ Date _____

Lesson 27
READER'S NOTEBOOK

The Dog That Dug
for Dinosaurs
Independent Reading

Reader's Guide

The Dog That Dug for Dinosaurs

Create a Fossil Hunting Guide

Use the text and illustrations to help Digger
complete a fossil hunting guide.

Read pages 425–426.
Describe fossils and
the tools needed to find them.

Read pages 427–428.
Explain to readers how to find fossils.

Name _____ Date _____

Read pages 434–435. Keep writing your fossil hunting guide. Tell your readers about some of the dangers of fossil hunting.

Read page 436. What kinds of fossils will people find?

Let readers of the fossil hunting guide know what to expect.

Words with *oo* as in *book*

Write the Basic Word that matches each clue.

Spelling Words

Basic Words
1. took
2. books
3. foot
4. hoof
5. cook
6. nook
7. hood
8. wood
9. stood
10. shook
11. crook
12. cookbook

1. Opposite of gave _____

2. To make food _____

3. Part of a coat that covers your head

_____

4. Things you read _____

5. A cow stands on this, but you don't.

_____

6. A small place to sit _____

7. Got up from sitting _____

8. You put a shoe over this.

_____

9. A book used to make food

_____

10. It comes from trees. _____

11. A person who steals _____

12. Wiggled all over _____

Lesson 27
READER'S NOTEBOOK

The Dog That Dug for Dinosaurs
Grammar: What Is an Adverb?

Adverbs and Adjectives

✎ **Draw a line under the adverb that tells how or when.**

1. Yesterday, we saw a show about dinosaurs.

2. We went there together.

3. We listened carefully to all the facts.

4. We took notes quietly.

5. Today, we are talking about the show.

6. Our teacher quickly lists the facts.

7. Tomorrow, we will write our papers.

8. Then, we will share our reports.

9. We will speak clearly.

10. The others will listen politely.

✎ **Choose the adverb or adjective that best completes each sentence. Underline it.**

11. We watched the dog run (quickly, quick) to the dirt area.

12. He was (careful, carefully) while digging for the old bones.

Shades of Meaning

Read the story. Complete each sentence by writing the word that fits better.

Tina and Larry went on a hike. They stopped at a creek

to _____ their lunch. Tina took her boots off.
  (eat   gobble)

She put her feet in the creek. "This feels good," she said. "The

water is _____."
  (freezing   cool)

"Look at that _____ animal," said
  (tiny   small)

Larry. "It's the size of a mouse. I think it's a chipmunk." He

_____ a peanut and tossed it to the chipmunk.
  (broke   smashed)

From the top of a hill, the children _____
  (saw   spotted)

another hiker. "Hey," said Tina, "that's Rob. He likes to hike

too." She _____ to get Rob's attention. Soon
  (screamed   yelled)

the three friends were hiking together.

"We should turn around," said Lawrence. "I'm

_____ we might not get home in time for dinner.
  (worried   scared)

I'm starving. I want to eat a _____ hamburger."
  (large   giant)

Proofread for Spelling

**Proofread the story. Circle the eight misspelled words.
Then write the correct spellings on the lines below.**

Spelling Words

1. took
2. books
3. foot
4. hoof
5. cook
6. nook
7. hood
8. wood
9. stood
10. shook
11. crook
12. cookbook

Review Words

13. look
14. good

    I had a funny dream. I dreamed I was sitting in a nook next to an old fireplace. I could smell the wud fire. Near the door, stud a huge cook. I knew because he wore an apron and held a cookbuck.

    He came over and shok my hand. Then he pulled a hood over his head and started cooking breakfast. It smelled gud. I saw that his right foat was not in a shoe, but was a huf! He smiled at me. He looked like a character from one of my story boaks!

1. _____   5. _____

2. _____   6. _____

3. _____   7. _____

4. _____   8. _____

Write these other Spelling Words in ABC order: *took, cook, nook, hood, look, crook.*

9. _____   12. _____

10. _____   13. _____

11. _____   14. _____

Using Adjectives

Circle the word that correctly completes the sentence.

1. I found (a, an) fossil today.

2. It is the (bigger, biggest) fossil I have ever seen.

3. It may be (a, an) leg bone of a dinosaur.

4. The other bone I found was (shorter, shortest).

Rewrite the paragraph. Add -<u>er</u> or -<u>est</u> to each underlined adjective. Write the new paragraph on the lines below.

I have the <u>great</u> dog in the world. His name is Chester. Chester digs in the park with his dog friends. Chester is <u>small</u> than his friend Chelsie, but he is the <u>fast</u> of all the dogs. He and his friend Luke find bones. The bone Chester finds is <u>long</u> than the others.

_____

_____

_____

_____

_____

_____

Connect to Writing

You can combine sentences that describe the same action. Use *and* to join the adverbs.

The tourists walked quickly. The tourists walked quietly.	The tourists walked quickly and quietly.
They are digging today. They are digging tomorrow.	They are digging today and tomorrow.

Read each pair of sentences. Use *and* to join the adverbs and write the new sentence.

1. We read about dinosaurs yesterday.
   We read about dinosaurs today.

   _____

2. I wrote my notes neatly.
   I wrote my notes carefully.

   _____

3. I'm going to study today.
   I'm going to study tomorrow.

   _____

4. I will answer the test questions slowly.
   I will answer the test questions correctly.

   _____

Words with *ow, ou*

Put these letters together to write words with *ow* and *ou*.
Then read each word aloud.

1. b + ow _____

2. c + l + ow + n _____

3. f + r + ow + n _____

4. l + ou + d _____

5. r + ou + n + d _____

**Now use the words you wrote above to complete the
sentences below.**

6. Bubbles the _____ came out
on the stage.

7. He blew up a big _____ balloon.

8. The balloon popped with a
_____ bang.

9. Bubbles had a big _____ on
his face.

10. Then Bubbles took a _____
while the crowd clapped.

Name _____ Date _____

Name _____ Date _____

Nouns Ending with *'s*

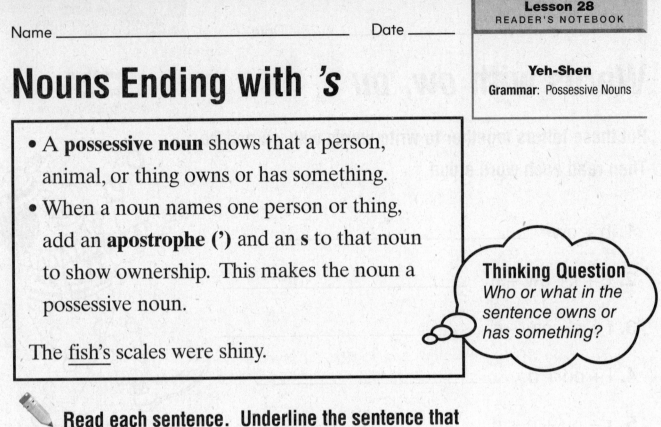

- A **possessive noun** shows that a person, animal, or thing owns or has something.
- When a noun names one person or thing, add an **apostrophe (')** and an **s** to that noun to show ownership. This makes the noun a possessive noun.

The <u>fish's</u> scales were shiny.

Thinking Question
Who or what in the sentence owns or has something?

Read each sentence. Underline the sentence that shows that a person owns or has something.

1. Yeh-Shen's mother and father had died.

   Yeh-Shens mother and father had died.

2. Her stepmother's cave was cold.

   Her stepmothers cave was cold.

3. The old mans advice was helpful.

   The old man's advice was helpful.

4. Her friends tail was beautiful.

   Her friend's tail was beautiful.

5. The kings men built a hut.

   The king's men built a hut.

Words with *ow, ou*

Word Bank

couch	crowd	crown	found	frown
howl	mouth	ouch	round	shout

Write a word from the box that matches each clue.

1. A part of your face _____

2. A sound a dog might make _____

3. A large group of people _____

4. A long seat for sitting _____

5. To yell loudly _____

6. Something a queen has _____

7. The shape of a ball _____

8. The face a grouch makes _____

9. What you say when you get hurt _____

10. Got something you were looking for _____

Yeh-Shen
Spelling: Words with *ow, ou*

Words with *ow, ou*

Sort the Spelling Words by the spellings *ow* and *ou*.

Spelling Words
Basic Words
1. cow
2. house
3. town
4. shout
5. down
6. mouse
7. found
8. loud
9. brown
10. ground
11. pound
12. flower
Review Words
13. out
14. now

ow Words

1. _____
2. _____
3. _____
4. _____
5. _____
6. _____

ou Words

7. _____
8. _____
9. _____
10. _____
11. _____
12. _____
13. _____
14. _____

Write the Spelling Words that rhyme with each given word.

15. how, _____, _____

16. blouse, _____, _____

17. clown, _____, _____, _____

18. bound, _____, _____, _____

Grade 2, Unit 6

Nouns Ending with s'

Yeh-Shen
Grammar: Possessive Nouns

- A **possessive noun** shows that a person, animal, or thing owns or has something.
- When a noun names more than one and ends in **s,** add just an **apostrophe (')** after the **s** to show ownership.

The <u>musicians'</u> show was great.

Thinking Question
Who or what in the sentence owns something?

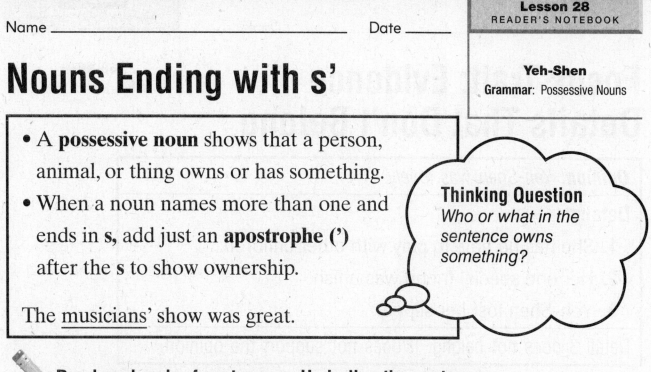

Read each pair of sentences. Underline the sentence that uses a possessive noun correctly.

1. Her parents death made Yeh-Shen an orphan.

Her parents' death made Yeh-Shen an orphan.

2. The dancers' costumes were colorful.

The dancers costumes were colorful.

3. The girls' dresses were beautiful.

The girls dresses were beautiful.

4. Her admirers praise made her happy.

Her admirers' praise made her happy.

5. The villagers' excitement grew.

The villagers excitement grew.

Focus Trait: Evidence
Details That Don't Belong

Opinion: Yeh-Shen was lonely.
Details:
1. She has no time to play with other children.
2. Her one special friend was a fish.
3. Yeh-Shen lost her slipper.
Detail 3 does not belong. It does not support the opinion.

Read each opinion and the details that follow. Cross out the detail that does not support the opinion.

1. **Opinion:** Jin should not have cooked Yeh-Shen's fish friend.

   Details: The fish meant a lot to Yeh-Shen.

   Jin went to the pond and caught the fish.

   Yeh-Shen's friendship with the fish did not keep her from doing her work.

2. **Opinion:** It was good that Yeh-Shen followed the old man's advice.

   Details: A traveler found Yeh-Shen's slipper.

   Yeh-Shen's wish was granted.

   The bones of the fish had special powers.

3. **Opinion:** The king's treatment of Jin and Jun-Li was too harsh.

   Details: Jin and Jun-Li could never come to the castle.

   Jin and Jun-Li had to stay in their cave.

   Jin and Jun-Li went to the festival.

Cumulative Review

Fill in the blanks.

1. It rhymes with **moss**.
It begins like **took**. _____

2. It rhymes with **moo**.
It begins like **cross**. _____

3. It rhymes with **book**.
It begins like **show**. _____

4. It rhymes with **room**.
It begins like **blue**. _____

5. It rhymes with **fawn**.
It begins like **yes**. _____

Now use words you wrote above to complete the sentences below.

6. Many flowers _____ in the spring.

7. A good _____ makes a ship
run smoothly.

8. When it got late, Tony started to _____.

Yeh-Shen

Write a Travel Brochure

Travelers want to take a tour and visit each place in Yeh-Shen's story. Tell why each place is important and draw a picture.

Read page 458.

The first stop on our tour is

_____

_____

_____

_____

Read pages 459–460.

The second stop on our tour is

_____

_____

_____

_____

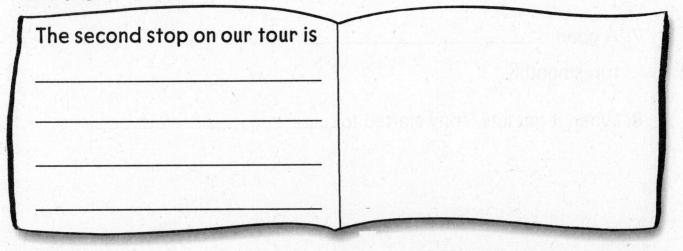

Read page 462–463.

The next stop on our tour is

_____

_____

_____

_____

Read page 464.

The last stop on our tour is

_____

_____

_____

_____

Think about the whole story.

After this tour, many
visitors say they have learned
an important lesson:

_____

_____

_____

Words with *ow, ou*

Write the Spelling Word that matches each clue.

Spelling Words

Basic Words
1. cow
2. house
3. town
4. shout
5. down
6. mouse
7. found
8. loud
9. brown
10. ground
11. pound
12. flower

Review Words
13. out
14. now

1. You can watch it bloom in the spring.

_____

2. When you call loudly, you

_____.

3. A _____ is smaller than a city.

4. The opposite of *lost* is _____.

5. You may live in one of these.

_____

6. A noise that hurts your ears is _____.

7. This tiny animal is afraid of cats. _____

8. The opposite of *in* is _____.

9. You get milk from a _____.

10. The opposite of *up* is _____.

Possessive Nouns

Yeh-Shen
Grammar: Possessive Nouns

> Underline the sentence that uses a possessive noun correctly for nouns that name one.

1. Her stepmother's demands were hard on Yeh-Shen.

Her stepmothers demands were hard on Yeh-Shen.

2. Yeh-Shen listened to the old mans advice.

Yeh-Shen listened to the old man's advice.

3. The girls wish came true.

The girl's wish came true.

4. The king's voice was full of kindness.

The kings voice was full of kindness.

> Underline the sentence that uses a possessive noun correctly for nouns that name more than one.

5. The slippers' size was very small.

The slippers size was very small.

6. The other girls' feet were too big.

The other girls feet were too big.

7. The soldiers job was hard.

The soldiers' job was hard.

8. The dancers movements were graceful.

The dancers' movements were graceful.

Classify and Categorize

Word Bank

prince	fairy godmother	stepsister
fish friend	king	girl
wise old man	traveler	

Read each word above. Write each word in the best category.

Characters in Fairy Tales	

Characters in Real Life	

Proofread for Spelling

Proofread the sentences. Circle the misspelled word. Then write the word correctly on the line.

Spelling Words

1. cow
2. house
3. town
4. shout
5. down
6. mouse
7. found
8. loud
9. brown
10. ground
11. pound
12. flower

1. When you see your present, you'll showt with joy!

   _____

2. Is that a stuffed mowse? _____

3. I have never seen a flouwer shop like that one!

   _____

4. That restaurant has the best waffles in toun.

   _____

5. I have never seen her howse. _____

6. All of his clothes are broun. _____

7. It takes a good caw to make good milk.

   _____

8. Come on doun to the kitchen for dinner!

   _____

9. I fownd the book that I lost. _____

10. She dropped her sandwich on the grownd.

    _____

Irregular Verbs

✏️ **Circle the word that correctly completes the sentence.**

1. Yeh-Shen (have, had) lots of chores.

2. She (do, did) her work well.

3. Yen-Shen (had, have) no help.

4. Jin and Jun-li (did, does) no work.

✏️ **Read the paragraph. Underline the six mistakes. Then rewrite the paragraph. Make sure each verb matches the subject in the sentence.**

    Long ago, Yeh-Shen have a hard life. Jin do mean things to her. Yeh-Shen have only rags to wear. She do chores all day. Then, Yeh-Shen have a wish. Her wish came true and at last she do a happy life.

_____

_____

_____

_____

_____

_____

Connect to Writing

Weak	Strong
The slippers belonging to Yeh-Shen were silk.	**Yeh-Shen's slippers** were silk.
The advice of the old man was good.	**The old man's advice** was good.

Rewrite each sentence. Use a possessive noun to rewrite each underlined group of words. Write the new sentences on the line.

1. The eyes belonging to the fish were golden.

_____

2. The stepmother of Yeh-Shen was angry.

_____

3. Yeh-Shen followed the directions of the old man.

_____

4. The men of the king caught Yeh-Shen.

_____

Reading Longer Words: Long Vowels *a* and *i*

Write a word from the box to complete each sentence.

Word Bank

frightened	pasted	kindly
racecar	higher	explained

1. The _____ woman likes to

   help her neighbors.

2. Dale's _____ was speeding

   around the track.

3. Dad _____ the problem in a

   way I could understand.

4. Were you _____ by the

   strange sounds in the middle of the night?

5. We watched the hot air balloon rise

   _____ in the sky.

6. Gina _____ the photos into

   her scrapbook.

Name _____ Date _____

Pronouns and Ownership

- A **possessive pronoun** shows that a person or animal owns or has something.

- *My*, *your*, *his*, and *her* come before a noun to show that someone has or owns something.

My <u>mom</u> gets two gifts.

Thinking Question
*What noun goes
with the pronoun?*

**Underline the possessive pronoun in each sentence.
Circle the noun that goes with it.**

1. His presents are on the table.

2. Mom also sees gifts from her children.

3. Her daughter gives two books.

4. Her son gives two flowers.

5. Mom opens your gifts, too.

6. My mom has a good birthday.

7. Her sister called this morning.

8. My dad will take her out to dinner tomorrow.

Reading Longer Words: Long Vowels *a* and *i*

Read each clue. Choose the answer from the word pair below.

1. Doing something to have fun _____

Water coming down from the sky _____

raining   **playing**

2. Talk about things that trouble you _____

Tell what something means _____

explain   **complain**

3. Flashes of light during a storm _____

Above something else _____

lightning   **higher**

4. A track that trains run on _____

A thing that plays music _____

railway   **radio**

5. Bright and glowing _____

Moving through the sky with wings _____

flying   **shining**

Name _____ Date _____

Lesson 29
READER'S NOTEBOOK

Two of Everything
Spelling: Words with
ai, ay, igh, y

Words with *ai, ay, igh, y*

Sort the Spelling Words by the spelling patterns.

Spelling Words

Long *a* Sound

1. _____
2. _____
3. _____
4. _____
5. _____
6. _____
7. _____
8. _____
9. _____

Long *i* Sound

10. _____
11. _____
12. _____
13. _____
14. _____

Basic Words

1. aim
2. snail
3. bay
4. braid
5. ray
6. always
7. gain
8. sly
9. chain
10. shy
11. bright
12. fright

Review Words

13. tray
14. try

Underline the letters in each word that stand for the long *a* or long *i* sound.

More Pronouns and Ownership

- Some **possessive pronouns** stand alone. They are usually at the end of a sentence.
- *Mine*, *yours*, *his*, and *hers* are possessive pronouns.

Which <u>coins</u> are **yours**?

Thinking Question
Which word shows that someone has or owns something?

Underline the possessive pronoun. Circle the noun that shows what is owned.

1. The pennies are mine.

2. The dimes are hers.

3. The quarters are his.

4. The nickels are yours.

5. The money is mine.

6. Which bank is yours?

7. That wallet is his.

8. The purse is hers.

9. The dollar is mine.

10. The coins are yours.

Focus Trait: Evidence Supporting Reasons

Good writers tell their opinions in responses to literature. They give reasons for their opinions. They support their reasons with examples from the story.

Read the opinion. Then read each reason that supports the opinion. Find an example from *Two of Everything* that supports each reason.

Opinion: The pot makes the Haktaks happy.

Reason	Example
1. The pot makes them rich.	
2. The pot helps them get a lot of things they did not have before.	
3. The pot makes them new friends.	
4. The pot helps them make other things they need.	

Words with *oi, oy*

Write the missing *oi* or *oy* word that will complete
each sentence.

Word Bank

joined	voice	cowboy
noise	enjoyed	spoiled

1. The _____ sat by the campfire.

2. He had a very nice _____ for singing.

3. He _____ singing to pass the time.

4. Sometimes the cows _____ in.

5. Their mooing _____ his songs.

6. The lovely singing became frightful _____.

**Read each word you wrote above. Write each one in the
correct column below, under the word that has the same
vowel spelling.**

point	toy
_____	_____
_____	_____
_____	_____
_____	_____

Reader's Guide

Two of Everything

Make a Cartoon

Make a cartoon to tell the story of Mr. and Mrs. Haktak.
Draw characters and write what they say.

Read pages 488–489.

Read pages 490–492.

Read pages 496–497.

Read pages 501–502.

Words with *ai, ay, igh, y*

Write the Spelling Word that means the same as the given word.

1. get _____

2. forever _____

3. a scare _____

4. sneaky _____

5. point _____

6. shiny _____

Write the Spelling Word that belongs in each group.

7. plate, platter, _____

8. slug, worm, _____

9. pigtail, ponytail, _____

10. quiet, timid, _____

11. beam, light, _____

12. attempt, effort, _____

13. rope, leash, _____

14. sea, harbor, _____

Spelling Words

Basic Words
1. aim
2. snail
3. bay
4. braid
5. ray
6. always
7. gain
8. sly
9. chain
10. shy
11. bright
12. fright

Review Words
13. tray
14. try

Name _____ Date _____

Possessive Pronouns

Underline the possessive pronoun in each sentence.
Circle the noun that goes with it.

1. Dana and Dan are my pals.

2. The twins help you with your homework.

3. Her help is with math.

4. His help is with reading.

5. My friends like to help people.

Underline the possessive pronoun in each sentence.
Circle the noun that goes with it.

6. The skates are mine.

7. The hats are yours.

8. The bats are his.

9. The balls are hers.

10. The tickets are mine.

Antonyms

Circle the antonyms in each sentence. Then write what each antonym means.

1. She put one purse into the pot and pulled out two.

   _____

2. They worked late filling and emptying the pot.

   _____

3. The branch swung high and low in the wind.

   _____

4. The tiny mouse wanted to be as huge as a horse.

   _____

5. The chair was heavy, but the pillows were light.

   _____

6. Mike was glad to have a rest, but Patty was unhappy.

   _____

7. Her dress was colorful, but her coat was faded.

   _____

Name _____   Date _____

Proofread for Spelling

Two of Everything
Spelling: Words with
ai, ay, igh, y

Proofread the paragraph. Circle the six misspelled words.
Then write the correct spellings on the lines below.

I am alwas late getting ready for school. My
mother says I am the only girl who actually does move
as slowly as a snayl. I take a long time to brade my hair,
and I brush my teeth over and over until they are
brite. Each day, I aym to move more quickly, but it
never quite works out. When I get to school, I have to
explain why I am late to my teacher. That is hard for me
because I am shi.

Spelling Words

Basic Words
1. aim
2. snail
3. bay
4. braid
5. ray
6. always
7. gain
8. sly
9. chain
10. shy
11. bright
12. fright

1. _____   4. _____

2. _____   5. _____

3. _____   6. _____

Unscramble the letters to write a Spelling Word.

7. yar _____

8. lys _____

9. nachi _____

10. inag _____

11. bya _____

12. firght _____

Grade 2, Unit 6

Irregular Verbs

Write each sentence. Use the past-tense verb.

1. Yesterday, dogs (run, ran) through the park.

_____

2. Two birds (come, came) after them.

_____

3. They (go, went) to the lake.

_____

4. They (see, saw) a giant rainbow.

_____

Replace each underlined word with a word from the box. Write the new sentences.

came	went	saw	ran

5. The boys <u>watched</u> two movies.

_____

6. They <u>walked</u> to two games.

_____

7. They <u>dashed</u> around the field.

_____

8. Then they <u>traveled</u> to my house.

_____

Connect to Writing

Weak	Strong
The teacher gave tests to the **teacher's** class.	The teacher gave tests to **her** class.
The student studied for the **student's** tests.	The student studied for **his** tests.

✏️ **Rewrite each paragraph. Replace the underlined words with the possessive pronoun** *mine, his, your,* **or** *her.*

  Miss Lee gave two tests today. Miss Lee got papers from <u>Miss Lee's</u> drawer.

  Miss Lee said to the students, "Take out <u>the students'</u> pencils."

  Dave took out <u>Dave's</u> green pencil. Annette picked up my blue pencil. I said, "That is <u>the one that belongs to me.</u>

_____

_____

_____

_____

_____

Reading Longer Words: Long *o* and *e*

Read the sentences. Draw a circle around each word that has the long *o* sound spelled *o, oa,* or *ow,* or the long *e* sound spelled *ee* or *ea.*

1. Rosa looked out the window on the coldest day of winter.

2. She noticed snowflakes floating down.

3. Slowly, the snow got deeper.

4. The snowplow went by on the street.

5. This might be the biggest snowstorm of the season.

Now write each word you circled under the word that has the same spelling for the same vowel sound.

folding	blowing	freezing
_____	_____	_____
_____	_____	_____
	_____	

coasting	_____	meaning
_____	_____	_____

Adjectives and Adverbs

- **Adjectives** are words that tell more about nouns.

  Ben Franklin had many <u>remarkable</u> talents.

- **Adverbs** are words that tell more about verbs.

  He played the harmonica <u>beautifully</u>.

Thinking Question
What word does the adjective or adverb tell more about?

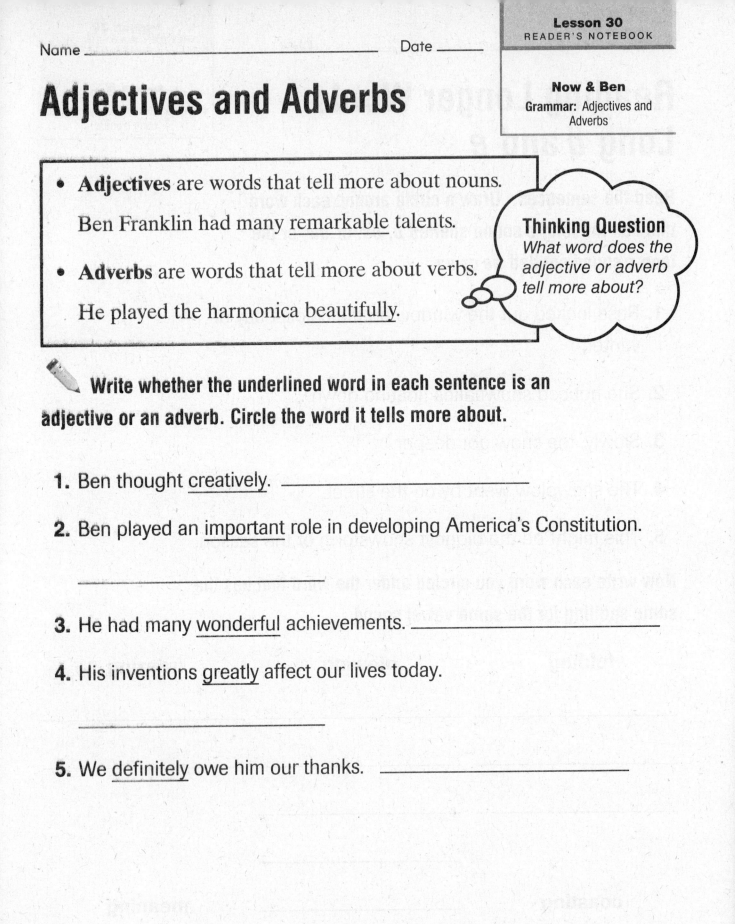

Write whether the underlined word in each sentence is an adjective or an adverb. Circle the word it tells more about.

1. Ben thought <u>creatively</u>. _____

2. Ben played an <u>important</u> role in developing America's Constitution.

_____

3. He had many <u>wonderful</u> achievements. _____

4. His inventions <u>greatly</u> affect our lives today.

_____

5. We <u>definitely</u> owe him our thanks. _____

Name _____ Date _____

Reading Longer Words: Long Vowels *o* and *e*

Fill in the blank.

1. We hiked up the hill on the

   _____ trail.

2. Tracey hit a _____ to win

   the game.

3. Do you have a good _____

   for being late?

4. Make a list of things we need on the

   _____.

5. Cupcakes are _____ than popcorn.

Word Bank

reason
steepest
sweeter
homerun
notepad

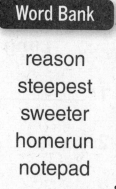

Read the words below. Think how the words in each group are alike. Write the missing word that will fit in each group.

6. morning, afternoon, _____

7. packing, filling, _____

8. door, wall, _____

9. moving away, going, _____

10. foam, bubbles, _____

Word Bank

loading
soapsuds
window
evening
leaving

Words with *oa, ow, ee, ea*

Sort the Spelling Words by the long *e* and long *o* vowel sounds.

Spelling Words

**Basic
Words**

Long *e* Sound	Long *o* Sound
1. _____	8. _____
2. _____	9. _____
3. _____	10. _____
4. _____	11. _____
5. _____	12. _____
6. _____	13. _____
7. _____	14. _____

1. seated
2. keeps
3. speed
4. seen
5. means
6. clean
7. groan
8. roast
9. bowls
10. crow
11. owe
12. grown

**Review
Words**

13. green
14. snow

Now sort the words by how the vowel sound is spelled.

Long *e* Spelled		Long *o* Spelled	
ee	*ea*	*oa*	*ow*
15. _____	19. _____	22. _____	24. _____
16. _____	20. _____	23. _____	25. _____
17. _____	21. _____		26. _____
18. _____			27. _____
			28. _____

Adjectives and Adverbs

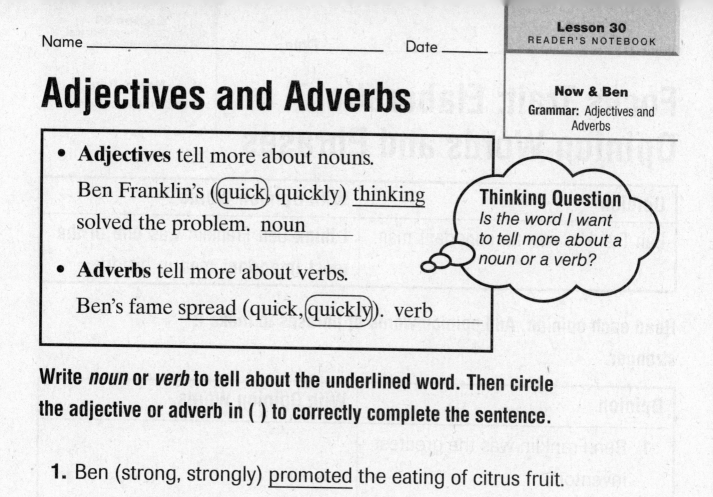

- **Adjectives** tell more about nouns.

  Ben Franklin's ((quick), quickly) <u>thinking</u>
  solved the problem. <u>noun</u>

- **Adverbs** tell more about verbs.

  Ben's fame <u>spread</u> (quick, (quickly)). <u>verb</u>

Thinking Question
*Is the word I want
to tell more about a
noun or a verb?*

Write *noun* or *verb* to tell about the underlined word. Then circle
the adjective or adverb in ( ) to correctly complete the sentence.

1. Ben (strong, strongly) <u>promoted</u> the eating of citrus fruit.

_____

2. He believed eating fruit would prevent an (awful, awfully) <u>disease</u>.

_____

3. Ben created (beautiful, beautifully) <u>music</u>.

_____

4. His music (deep, deeply) <u>moved</u> many composers.

_____

5. Many people (great, greatly) <u>appreciated</u> Ben's achievements.

_____

Focus Trait: Elaboration
Opinion Words and Phrases

Opinion	With Opinion Words
Ben Franklin was an important man.	**I think** Ben Franklin was **one of the most important** men in history.

Read each opinion. Add opinion words or phrases to make it stronger.

Opinion	With Opinion Words
1. Ben Franklin was the greatest inventor.	
2. Ben Franklin's hospital made his city better.	
3. The documents that Ben Franklin helped to write were very important.	
4. Ben Franklin's work in the past is important for our future.	

Final Stable Syllable *-le*

Read the clues. Then write one of the two words below each clue in the blank.

1. A kind of dog _____

A horn for making music _____

beagle   **bugle**

2. A sweet, crunchy fruit _____

To eat in small bites _____

nibble   **apple**

3. Used for mending clothes _____

A soft food in some soups _____

noodle   **needle**

4. Easy to do _____

Peaceful or kind _____

gentle   **simple**

5. Burned to give light _____

A small pool of rainwater _____

candle   **puddle**

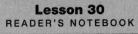

Now and Ben

Make a Drawing and Label It

Imagine that Ben Franklin made a time machine and traveled into our time. Make a sketch of some of his inventions that we still use. Write a sentence explaining to him how each invention has changed.

Read pages 528–529. Suppose Ben saw a swimmer practicing with flippers and fins.

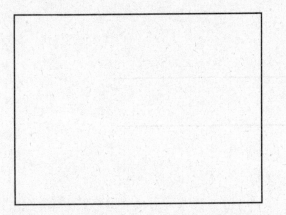

```
┌──────────────┐    _____
│              │
│              │    _____
│              │
│              │    _____
│              │
└──────────────┘    _____
```

Read pages 532. Suppose Ben saw a school with a desk and chair.

```
┌──────────────┐    _____
│              │
│              │    _____
│              │
│              │    _____
│              │
└──────────────┘    _____
```

Read page 534. Suppose Ben saw an odometer on a car.

Read page 535. Suppose Ben saw a library.

Words with *oa, ow, ee, ea*

Write the Basic Word that matches each clue.

1. in a chair _____

2. large black bird _____

3. how fast you move _____

4. to cook in an oven _____

5. not dirty _____

6. a croaking or unhappy sound

_____

Write the Basic Word that completes each sentence.

7. Milk spilled when the cereal _____

   fell off the table.

8. I _____ my brother 25 cents.

9. When I am _____, I will be much

   taller.

10. I have never _____ an eagle.

Spelling Words

Basic Words

1. seated
2. keeps
3. speed
4. seen
5. means
6. clean
7. groan
8. roast
9. bowls
10. crow
11. owe
12. grown

Review Words

13. green
14. snow

Name _____ Date _____

Lesson 30
READER'S NOTEBOOK

Now & Ben
Grammar: Adjectives and
Adverbs

Adjectives and Adverbs

- **Adjectives** are words that tell about nouns.
- **Adverbs** are words that tell about verbs.

Ben was a (careful, carefully) swimmer.

Ben put on the flippers (careful, carefully).

Write *noun* or *verb* to tell about the underlined word.
Then circle the adjective or adverb to correctly complete
each sentence.

1. Many people admired Ben (great, greatly).

_____

2. Ben solved problems (quick, quickly).

_____

3. Ben created (useful, usefully) inventions.

_____

4. Some of Ben's work was (dangerous, dangerously).

_____

5. Ben shared his inventions (eager, eagerly).

_____

Root Words

Underline the root word in each word. Use what you know
about the root word to figure out the word's meaning.
Complete each sentence by writing the word whose meaning
fits best.

> **Vocabulary**
>
> western   toaster   reheat   strongest
> undone   writer   stinky   unearth

1. I tripped because my shoelaces were

_____.

2. "That dog is _____," said Ms.

Petersen. "She needs a bath."

3. Jose saw a beautiful rainbow in the

_____ sky.

4. A _____ told the class how she

gets ideas for her stories.

5. If we dig here, I bet we'll _____

a treasure.

6. "Please put my bread in the _____,"

said Sophie's father.

7. Hank is the _____ batter on the team.

He hit six homeruns.

8. The soup is cold, so we must _____ it.

Proofread for Spelling

**Proofread the postcard. Circle the six misspelled words.
Then write the correct spellings on the lines below.**

Dear Tomas,

    You would not believe the things we have
sean on our trip. We went to a place where potters make
clay boals big enough to sit in! Can you imagine being
seeted in a pot? Each pattern meens something different.
If a crowe is painted, it is for good luck. I hope the town
keaps making the pottery so you can see it someday.

                    Manny

1. _____	4. _____
2. _____	5. _____
3. _____	6. _____

Unscramble the letters to write a Spelling Word.

7. angro _____

8. weo   _____

9. despe _____

10. leanc _____

11. stoar _____

12. rowng _____

Spelling Words

**Basic
Words**
1. seated
2. keeps
3. speed
4. seen
5. means
6. clean
7. groan
8. roast
9. bowls
10. crow
11. owe
12. grown

**Review
Words**
13. green
14. snow

Irregular Verbs

✏️ **Underline the correct verb to finish each sentence. Use the clue that tells when the action happens.**

1. We (give, gave) reports today.   **Now**

2. I (take, took) the topic of Ben Franklin.   **Past**

3. Sara and I (eat, ate) lunch.   **Past**

4. The teacher (say, said) I could give my report first.   **Past**

✏️ **Read this story about something that happened last week. Write the underlined words correctly. Use verbs that tell about the past.**

   I eat lunch with my sister. She give me a library book. It was about Ben Franklin. She say she liked it. I take the book to my room. It was a good book. Ben Franklin give the world many things. It take me just a little while to read the book.

_____

_____

_____

_____

Connect to Writing

> - **Adjectives** tell more about nouns.
>   He heard the <u>loud</u> thunder.
>
> - **Adverbs** tell more about verbs.
>   He prepared his equipment <u>carefully</u>.

Write *noun* or *verb* to tell about the underlined word.
Then circle the adjective or adverb in ( ) to correctly
complete the sentence.

1. It <u>rained</u> (heavy, heavily).

_____

2. (Bright, Brightly) <u>lightning</u> lit up the sky.

_____

3. Ben Franklin had a (bold, boldly) <u>idea</u>.

_____

4. His <u>plan</u> was (dangerous, dangerously).

_____

5. His experiment <u>worked</u> (perfect, perfectly).

_____

Name _____ Date _____

Unit 6
READER'S NOTEBOOK

Exploring Space Travel
Segment 1
Independent Reading

Reader's Guide

Exploring Space Travel

Be an Astronaut!

Read page 12. Imagine you're an astronaut
on the Soyuz. The Soyuz has three modules.
Write notes that tell about each module.

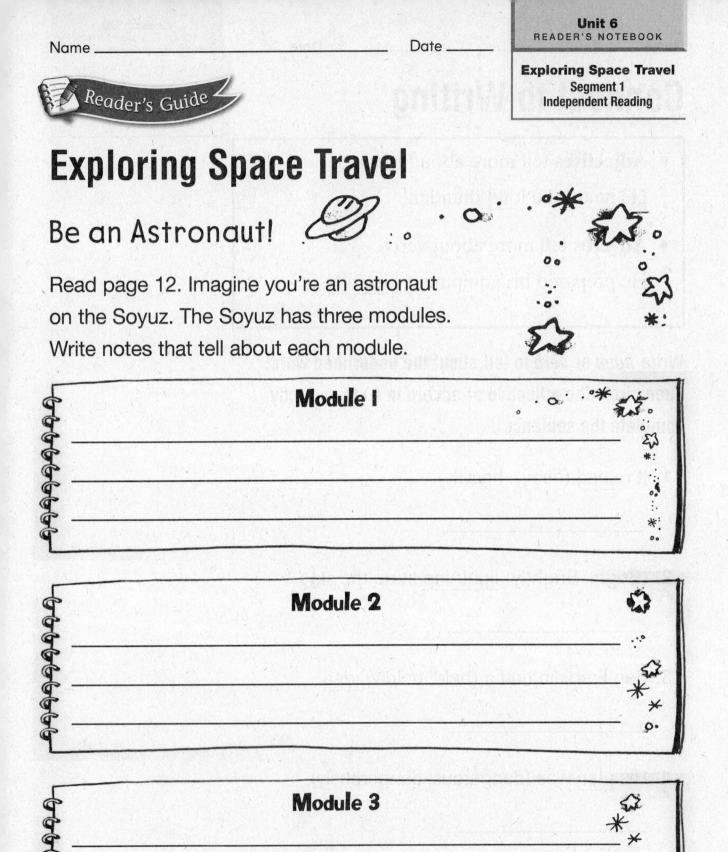

Module 1

_____

_____

_____

Module 2

_____

_____

_____

Module 3

_____

_____

_____

Name _____ Date _____

Use the picture on page 12 to help you draw a diagram of the Soyuz spacecraft. Then write the module numbers and use your notes to tell how the astronauts use each module. After you write, draw a line connecting the writing to each module.

Module _____

_____

_____

_____

Module _____

_____

_____

_____

_____

Module _____

_____

_____

_____

_____

Name _____   Date _____

Unit 6
READER'S NOTEBOOK

Exploring Space Travel
Segment 2
Independent Reading

Reader's Guide

Exploring Space Travel

Make Checklists

Wow! Astronauts have a lot to remember.
Complete the table to help the astronauts
remember when to wear their special suits
and clothes. Use the text, photos, and
captions in Chapters 3 and 4 to help you.

When	What to Wear
During takeoff and landing	
On spacewalks	
In the spacecraft when working	

Name _____ Date _____

Unit 6
READER'S NOTEBOOK

Exploring Space Travel
Segment 2
Independent Reading

There is no gravity in the spacecraft. Objects and people are weightless. Make a checklist to remind astronauts how to stay safe without gravity. Add details to tell them why.

When	What to Do
Eating	
Sleeping	
Working	

Name _____   Date _____

Reader's Guide

Exploring Space Travel

Become an Astronaut!

Read pages 29–37. Think about what people have to do so they can become astronauts. Make a web that shows four things a person must do to become an astronaut.

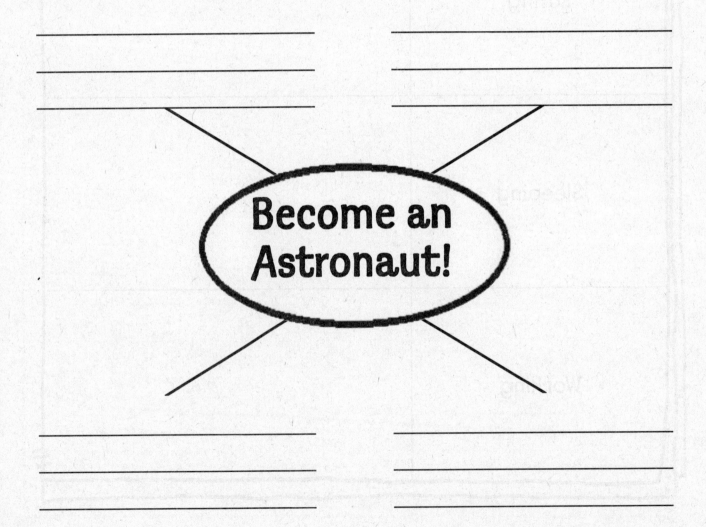

_____   _____
_____   _____

Become an Astronaut!

_____   _____
_____   _____

Name _____ Date _____

Look back at your web. Use those facts to make an ad that will tell people how to become an astronaut. Remember that an ad should be exciting to get people's attention.

Become an Astronaut!

_____

_____

_____

_____

_____

Reading and Writing Glossary

Use this glossary to help you remember and use words that you are learning about reading and writing.

A

abbreviation A short way to write a word by taking out some of the letters and adding a period at the end.

adjective A word that describes a noun. An adjective may tell how something looks, tastes, smells, sounds, or feels.

adverb A word that describes a verb. An adverb may tell how, where, when, or how much something is. An adverb may end in *-ly*.

alphabetical order When words are listed in the same order as the letters of the alphabet.

analyze To look at or study something carefully.

antonym A word that has the opposite, or nearly the opposite, meaning as another word.

apostrophe A punctuation mark (') that takes the place of missing letters in a word.

author's purpose The reason an author has for writing a text.

B

bar graph A drawing that uses bars to compare numbers.

base word A word to which endings, prefixes, and suffixes can be added. A base word is also called a root word.

biography A story that tells about the real events that make up a person's life.

boldface print Dark print that stands out from the rest of a text.

C

....

caption Text that gives more information about a photograph.

categorize To name a group of similar objects.

cause The reason why something happens.

characters The people and animals in a story.

chart A drawing that lists information in a clear way.

classify To group similar objects.

command A type of sentence that gives an order. A command may end with a period (.) or an exclamation mark (!).

compare To tell how things are alike.

compound sentence A sentence made up of two shorter sentences. A compound sentence is connected by words such as *and, but,* and *or.*

compound word A longer word made up of two shorter words.

conclusion An idea or opinion reached after thinking about several facts.

connect To link things that are similar.

context The words and sentences around a word that give readers clues to its meaning.

contraction A short way of writing two words using an apostrophe (').

contrast To tell how things are different.

D

detail A fact or example that tells more about a main idea.

diagram A drawing that shows how something works.

dialogue A conversation between two or more characters in a story.

dictionary entry A book part that lists a word with its correct pronunciation, part of speech, and meaning.

directions Step-by-step instructions for how to do or make something.

E

effect Something that happens as a result of something else.

electronic menu A feature of a website that lists the information that can be found on the website.

ending A word part attached to the end of a base word (or root word) that can change the meaning of the base word.

evaluate To form an opinion or make a judgment about something.

exclamation A sentence that shows a strong feeling. An exclamation begins with a capital letter and ends with an exclamation point (!).

F

fable A short story in which a character learns a lesson.

fact Something that can be proved true.

fairy tale A make-believe story that has been told for many years.

fantasy A story that could not happen in real life.

folktale A type of traditional tale.

formal language The kind of words and sentences that should be used when writing or speaking in school or with someone you do not know well.

future tense The form of a verb that tells about an action that will happen in the future.

G

glossary A list of unfamiliar or specialized words with their definitions, usually found at the back of a book.

graphic features Photographs or drawings, including maps and charts, that stand for ideas or add details to the text.

H

heading The title of part of a text.

homograph A word that has the same spelling as another word but has a different meaning and may be pronounced differently.

homophone A word that sounds the same as another word but is spelled differently and has a different meaning.

humorous fiction A story that includes characters who do or say funny things. Humorous fiction may also include events that would not happen in real life.

I

icon A symbol or picture on a website.

idiom A saying or expression that cannot be understood from the individual meanings of the words that make it up or by its literal meaning.

illustration A drawing that shows important details to help the reader understand more about the story.

informal language A casual way of using words and sentences when writing or speaking to friends or family members.

informational text Text that gives facts about real events and people.

informative writing Writing that gives facts about a topic.

interview A conversation in which a person asks another person questions and records his or her answers.

L

label Text that points out an important part of a diagram or other picture.

M

main idea The most important idea about the topic.

map A drawing of a town, state, or other place.

moral The lesson a character learns in a story.

multiple-meaning word A word that has more than one meaning.

N

narrative nonfiction Text that tells a true story about a topic.

narrative writing Writing that tells a story. A narrative tells about something that happened to a person or a character.

noun A word that names a person, an animal, a place, or a thing.

O

opinion What someone thinks, believes, or feels.

opinion writing Writing that tells what the writer believes and gives reasons.

P

past tense The form of a verb that tells about an action that happened in the past.

photograph A real-life image, taken with a camera, that can help to show ideas in a text.

play A story that people act out.

plot The order of story events, including the problem and how it is solved.

plural noun A noun that names more than one person, animal, place, or thing.

poetry Text that is written in a special way to use rhythm and the sound of the words to show ideas and feelings.

point of view The way a character or person thinks about an event.

possessive noun A noun that shows a person or animal owns or has something.

possessive pronoun A pronoun that shows ownership, such as *my, your, mine, yours, his,* and *hers.*

predicate The part of the sentence where the verb is found. The predicate tells what the subject did or does.

prefix A word part attached at the beginning of a base word (or root word) that changes the meaning of the word.

present tense The form of a verb that tells about an action happening now, in present time.

pronoun A word that can take the place of a noun, such as *I, he, she, it, we,* or *they.*

proper noun A special name of a person, animal, place, or thing. A proper noun begins with a capital letter.

Q

question A type of sentence that asks something and ends with a question mark (?).

quotation marks Punctuation marks that show what someone says. Quotation marks (" ") are placed at the beginning and end of a speaker's exact words.

R

realistic fiction A story that could happen in real life.

reflexive pronoun A special pronoun, such as *myself, himself, herself, themselves,* and *ourselves,* that is used after a verb.

repetition A pattern of writing in which the same words are used more than once.

research report Writing that tells what a writer learned from doing research about a topic.

rhythm A pattern of beats. The musical notes, words, and phrases in a song make up its rhythm.

root word A simple word that is part of another word. It is also known as a base word. Adding a prefix or suffix to a root word changes its meaning.

S

sequence of events The order in which things happen.

setting When and where a story takes place.

simile A comparison that uses *like* or *as.*

simple sentence A short sentence with a subject and predicate. Two simple sentences joined by a comma and a word such as *and, but,* or *or* make up a compound sentence.

singular noun A noun that names one person, animal, place, or thing.

song Words and music that are sung together.

statement A type of sentence that tells something and ends with a period (.).

story structure The way characters, a setting, and a plot are put together in a story.

subheading A short title that gives more information about a selection. A subheading comes after a selection's heading.

subject The naming part of a sentence, which tells who or what did or does something.

suffix A word part attached to the end of a base word that changes the meaning of the word.

synonym A word that has the same, or almost the same, meaning as another word.

T

text and graphic features Photographs, labels, headings, captions, illustrations, dark print, and other special features that add information to a selection.

text evidence Clues in the words and pictures that help you figure things out.

text features Parts of the text, such as headings or boldface print, that help readers recognize important information.

time line A drawing that shows the order in which events happened.

topic What a text is mainly about.

traditional tale A story that has been told for many years.

traits Ways of speaking and acting that show what someone is like.

V

verb A word that names an action that someone or something does or did. A verb can also tell what someone or something is.

W

website An online collection of pages about a topic.

word choice The words and phrases an author uses to make his or her writing interesting and clear.